MORE SUBROUTINE SANDWICH

MORE SUBROUTINE SANDWICH

Dr. John P. Grillo
Dr. J. D. Robertson

Bentley College

John Wiley & Sons, Inc.
New York • Chichester • Brisbane • Toronto • Singapore

Publisher: Judy V. Wilson
Editor: Dianne Littwin
Managing Editor: Maria Colligan
Composition & Make-up: Cobb/Dunlop Publisher Services Inc.

Library of Congress Cataloging in Publication Data

Grillo, John P.
More subroutine sandwich.

Includes index.

1. Electronic digital computers—Programming.
2. Basic (Computer program language) I. Robertson, J. D. (James Douglas), 1943– . II. Title.
QA76.6.G748 1982 001.64'25 82-13506
ISBN 0-471-86921-X

Printed in the United States of America

83 84 10 9 8 7 6 5 4 3 2 1

To Olivia

CONTENTS

PREFACE

Microcomputers have generated a lot of frustration for the individuals who own them. This disenchantment is often caused by the user's inability to tap the microcomputer's real power. Their hardware is either underused, perhaps only to play games, or misused if it performs tasks like telephone number management that could be done more simply by hand.

Even so, the popular press has had a field day. It has glorified the young entrepreneurs who have evidenced imagination, a good sense for a user's need, and a deep knowledge of computer programming by writing and marketing highly popular business and game programs. These *nouveaux riches* of technology have capitalized on an old idea: To solve a problem, first you must understand it fully, then you must analyze it, or break it up into its component parts.

It is this process of splitting a problem into its modules that leads directly to the use of subroutines. Any subroutine is, after all, neither more nor less than an isolated piece of the overall problem. This book is designed as a reference work to supply the programmer with a selection of problem modules. It is still the programmer's challenge to discover the user's need and to design the complete program.

The material in this book is divided into three parts. Parts I and III are the slices of bread; the subroutines in Part II are the filling for this sandwich between these two slices. The first part should be read sequentially to understand how to use the book and its contents. Part II is the meat (salami? tuna fish? corned beef?) of the matter. It could be useful to scan its contents once, to get the feel of its structure. However, we see its primary use to be a pool of subroutines from which you sample the desired modules according to need.

In the third part of the book we provide you with five larger programs, each incorporating one or more of the subroutines that we enclosed in the central section. Some of these programs are at the level of commercial applications for which you could be expected to pay twenty to a hundred dollars each. We thought it more important to enrich this volume with demonstration applications rather than to try to capitalize on these programs separately.

There may be some readers who wish we could have included more explanation of how these subroutines work. For these readers we have provided a starting point, a reference that will answer that need. However, we feel very strongly that you do not have to know exactly how a tool or appliance works in order to use it. Very few microcomputer owners know how their hardware works. You don't need to know how a sort works so long as you know that it arranges a list. You know its function and that's enough to answer the need.

We wish to thank the many friends and colleagues for their suggestions and manuscript reviews. We also wish to express our gratitude to the staff of John Wiley & Sons, particularly to Dianne Littwin, for their helpful cooperation.

PART I

Suggestions to the Reader

Introduction

The structure of this book is substantially different from that of the usual text or reference book. To enclose a set of subroutines between two covers is obviously not enough. You, the reader, should expect to be treated with more than a simple accumulation of BASIC statements.

The first two chapters comprising Part One are intended to familiarize you with the book's structure and with its application to your programming problems. Chapter 1 suggests some techniques on how to develop an application using this book. Chapter 2 details more specifically how to incorporate a subroutine into your BASIC program.

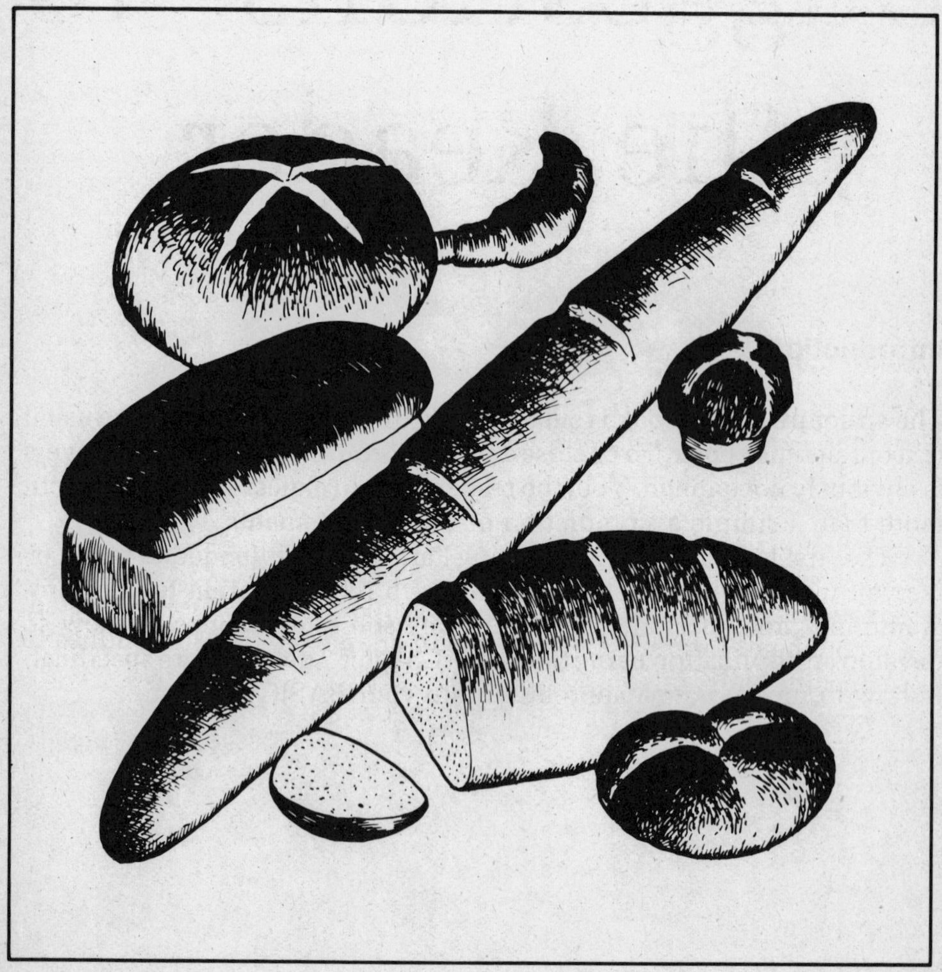

CHAPTER

1

HOW TO USE THIS BOOK

Using the Software in This Book

This is the second volume of subroutines gathered together as a "sandwich" between two "appetizing" covers. The 36 subroutines in the first book, which we called "Subroutine Sandwich," were only the beginning. Those 36 subroutines together with the 36 subroutines in this volume are in constant use both in and out of the classroom, so they are well tested. We recommend that you lose no time in adapting these subroutines to your specific programs.

Many of these subroutines have been developed by computer programmers from methods that existed in other disciplines. Our contribution is primarily one of synthesis and accumulation into one place, and translation into one version of one computer language.

User Friendliness

For the past two dozen or so years, the computer industry has undergone several major evolutionary changes. First and most obvious has been the changing electronic technology, which has resulted in hardware cost and size reductions without compromises in performance. Another major change has involved the system software—operating systems and language processors such as BASIC and Pascal. The result has been the evolution of "user-friendly" computers that communicate with people in nonthreatening terms.

Yet another change in the industry has been in the area of applications software—that is, the programs written to solve specific problems in a wide variety of user environments. For example, a computerized auto parts inventory system uses related programs to solve the auto parts retailer's inventory problems.

Some examples of application programs for which a microcomputer could be appropriate are:

For the home:

- *stereo record information system*
- *household goods insurance inventory*
- *TV movie information storage*
- *income tax preparation*
- *household energy audit*
- *computer games*

For a small business:

- *parts inventory*
- *payroll*
- *accounts receivable, payable*
- *general ledger*
- *market trend analysis*
- *salesperson performance*

This last area of change, applications software, interests us most. It is the one that most heavily influences the newest computer user, the microcomputer owner.

Program Planning

When you program in BASIC, whether it is on a TRS-80 or on some other computer, you are usually writing an application program, which is a program intended to solve a specific problem in an area of interest—perhaps statistics, or business, or word processing.

In order to compose and test your program effectively, you must plan your sequence of activities carefully. For instance, suppose that you want to write a program that organizes your stereo record collection. You need to establish your activities in a sequence, such as:

- *determine the information to be stored and retrieved*
- *design displays and reports from the computer*
- *outline the input dialog*
- *design the record storage system*
- *produce the overall program design*
- *write the BASIC modules*
- *test the program with typical data*
- *enter all data*
- *use and modify when necessary*

The wrong thing to do is to sit at the computer and say to yourself, "Now to write the program!" without first producing some organized notes or a sketched-out program on paper.

Remember that you can see only 12 to 24 lines of code on the screen (16 on the TRS-80 screen) at any one time. You can work this limitation to your advantage by planning your program in modules, or small segments, so that each section of the program tends to stand alone and performs a single given task.

You might subdivide the stereo record information system above into this set of modules:

- *add a new record's information*
- *delete an old record*
- *delete an entire file*
- *modify an existing record*
- *sort the names according to composer*
– *conductor*
– *performer*
– *label*
- *produce a report on the screen*
– *on the printer*

Modular Programming

If the preceding section sounds a lot like some kind of justification for modular programming using subroutines, so much the better. That is its intent. We are convinced that if you attack all programming tasks with this approach, you will be a better programmer for it. After all, structured programming techniques, of which modular programming is one aspect, have saved large corporations many millions of dollars. Modular programming will save you time.

In the classroom, we make a point of teaching our students the essential features of modular programming, especially as used in conjunction with top-down program design principles. Top-down design implies an approach to problem solution rather than a rigorous use of technical tools. It is more a philosophy than a procedure. It requires that you think of your problem in its most global, all-encompassing sense first. Design the entire problem in rough form.

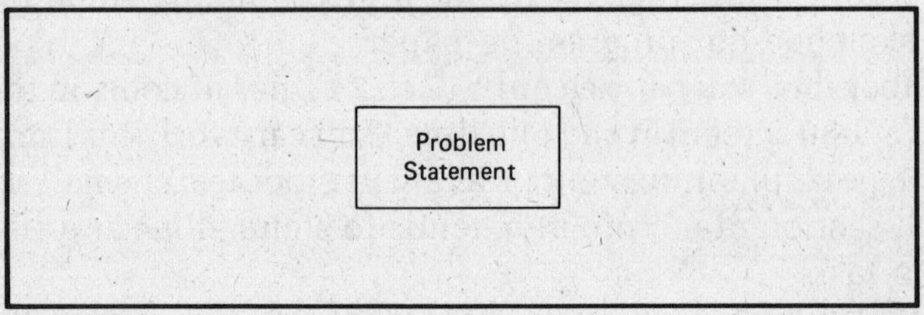

Then subdivide that huge problem into several major parts, usually three or four. Design each of these into more and more detail.

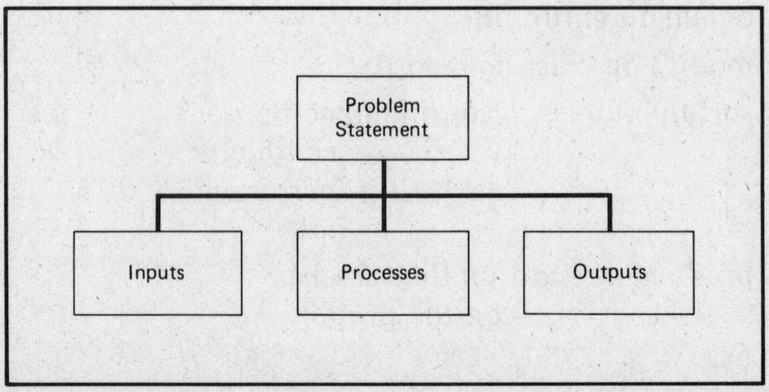

Continue to subdivide, one level of complexity at a time, until the whole problem is outlined in the form of a pyramid.

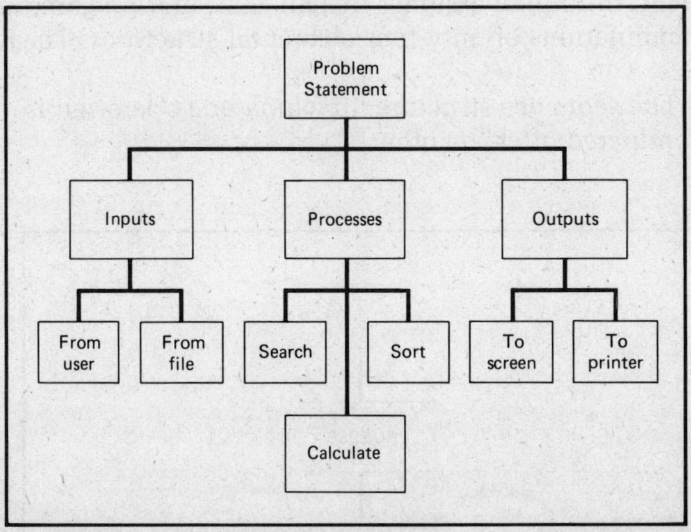

You will recognize this approach as similar to the one you use when you outline a theme or essay. First you describe the entire topic. Then you divide it into its major parts. Then you subdivide each major part into its minor parts.

We encourage our students to use GOSUBs to as-yet-unwritten routines so that if their problem is too big in scope they can plan to incorporate those unwritten modules later. This planned delay often makes it possible for them to get the skeletal parts of the program written. Later, as they mature in their understanding of the problem, they can code and test separately the subroutine that was the stumbling block. If they still have difficulty, we suggest a further modularization of the subroutine into even smaller parts, each of which is more easily understandable and capable of being coded and tested separately.

Structured Programming

Structured programming is a name given to a popular approach to computer problem solution. It assumes that all computer programs are composed of combinations of only four elemental structures. These are:

> – *The sequence structure, in which one operation is conducted after the other.*

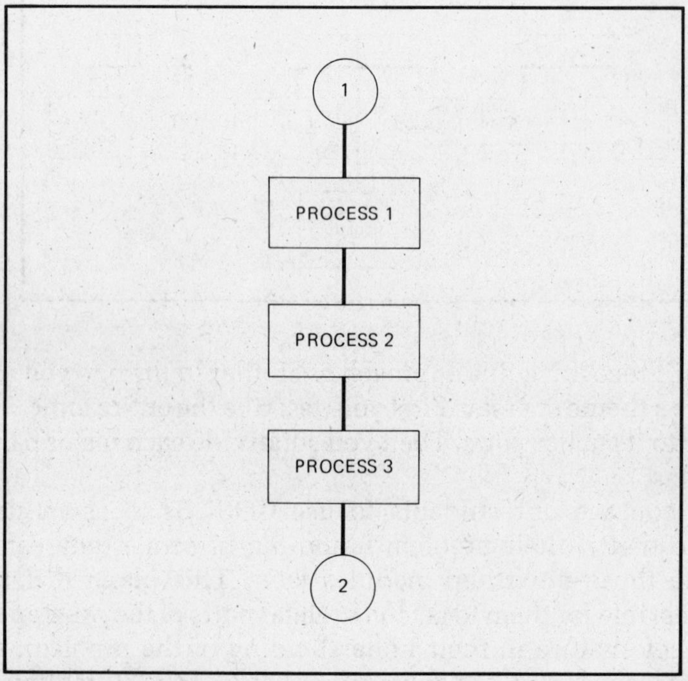

Sequence Structure

> – *The decision structure, in which a choice of two operations (or series of operations) is made depending on whether a condition is true or false.*

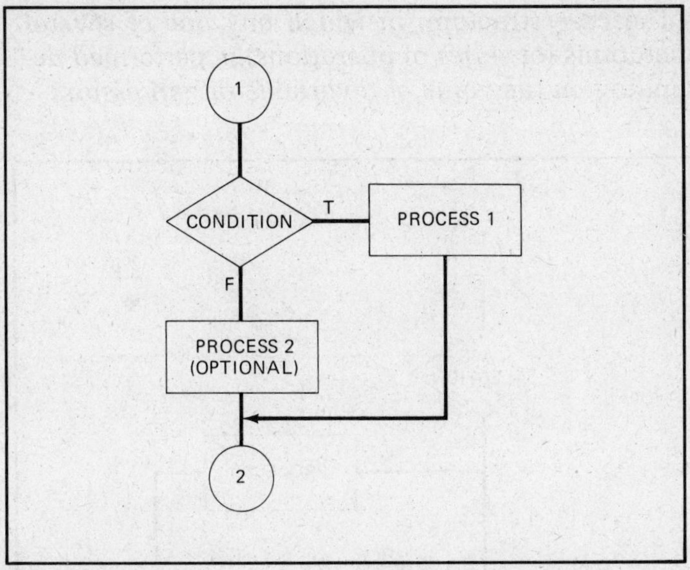

Decision Structure

– The loop structure, in which an operation (or series of operations) is performed repeatedly. There are two fundamental types of loop structures: If the condition is tested first, it is called a DO-WHILE. If the condition is tested last, it is called a DO-UNTIL.

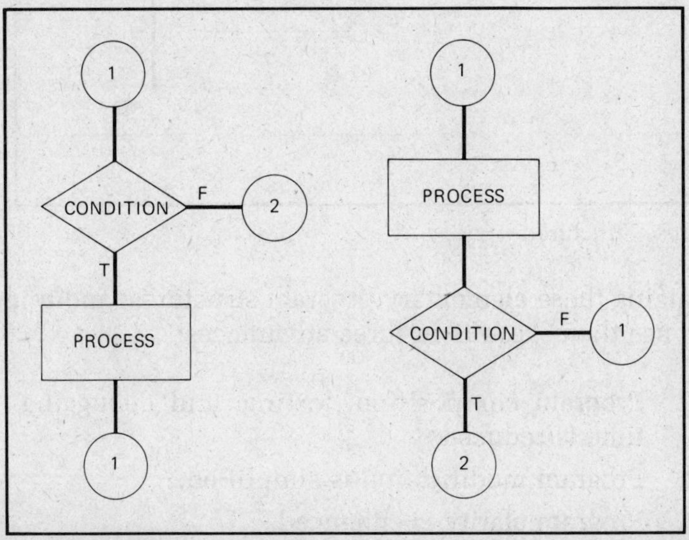

Loop Structures

– *The case structure, in which any one of several operations (or series of operations) is performed depending on the value of a variable or expression.*

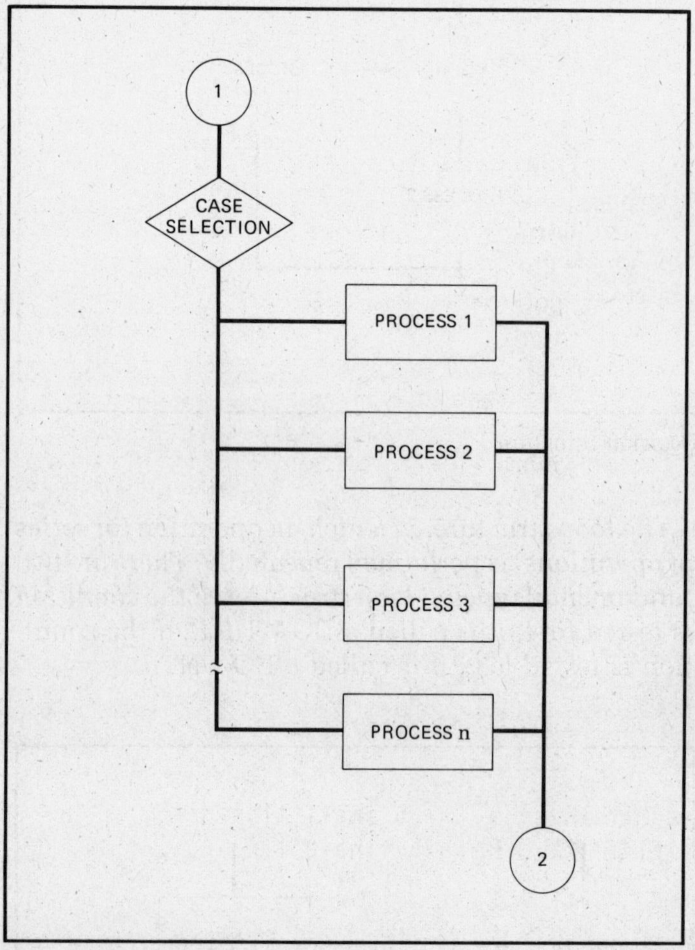

Case Structure

Recognizing these elementary program structures, and understanding how to use them, results in three advantages:

1. Program composition, testing, and debugging time is reduced.
2. Program modification is simplified.
3. Program clarity is enhanced.

The last point, program clarity, is very important. Note that if a program is to have value, it must "live" a long time and be amenable to change by its various readers.

Enhanced BASIC

The BASIC language has evolved, as have most computer languages, into several substantially different and more powerful versions. Most of these newer versions of BASIC have in common many extensions to the original version, and so they are called collectively either extended BASIC or enhanced BASIC.

You can write structured programs in BASIC on the TRS-80 with a minimum of effort. The language lends itself to the composition of modules, to GOTO-less code, to easily modifiable programs, through several powerful enhancements to standard BASIC.

ON-GOSUB

This instruction allows a case structure without GOTOs. This is especially useful when you have a menu-driven program, allowing the user to select one activity for the computer to perform among a list, or menu, of choices.

IF-THEN-ELSE

With this form of the branch, you can show explicitly the tasks that are to be performed based on a condition. A typical form of this statement is

```
IF (condition)
  THEN GOSUB (subroutine-1 line-no)
  ELSE GOSUB (subroutine-2 line-no)
```

Multiple statements per line

This construct lets you take care of several tasks, say within a THEN or ELSE clause. For example, study this form:

```
IF (condition)
  THEN (do this): (do this): (do this)
  ELSE (do that): (do that): (do that)
```

Notice how clear this structure is. Compare it with the convoluted GOTO-full code you would be forced to write if you didn't have multiple statements per line.

```
        IF (condition) THEN (line-no-X)
         (do that)
         (do that)
         (do that)

         GOTO (line-no-Y)
(line-no-X)    (do this)
               (do this)
               (do this)
(line-no-Y)
         ...
```

Algorithms

An algorithm is a step-by-step series of instructions for solving a particular problem. It must be

> – *effective—that is, it must solve the problem*
>
> – *finite—that is, it must do so in a reasonable amount of time*
>
> – *unambiguous—that is, it cannot leave any room for doubt as to what has to be done next*

A common example of an algorithm is the one below. The problem is to call a friend on the telephone.

1. Get friend's number.
2. Lift receiver to ear.
3. If no dial tone, stop because you can't call out.
4. If dial tone, dial friend's number.
5. If busy signal, go to step 11.
6. If it rings, start counting rings.
7. If it rings 7 times, go to step 11.
8. If it is answered by your friend, go to step 12.
9. If it is answered by another person, ask whether your friend is home.
10. If friend is home, wait for him or her to get to the phone, then go to step 12.
11. Hang up and try again later.
12. Talk to your friend. Success!

We are especially concerned with the antiquated notion that computer programming is a secret art form, that you have to "pay your dues" as an error-prone apprentice before you can become competent. We feel strongly that good programming is mostly the result of your recognition of user's need, not your skill at bit-fiddling or fancifying code. When you write a program, you spend a lot of time trying to figure out a method for doing this or that; in other words, you spend time designing and coding the module's algorithm.

Our intent is to provide you with a set of subroutines you can insert into your programs with a minimum of effort. We have used and tested these in a wide variety of situations on several different computers in as many as three different languages. After all, it's the method of solution, the algorithm, that's hard to develop. The code is a simple task by comparison.

Hardware Used

Although this book was intended primarily for the TRS-80 BASIC programmer, it is appropriate for any other programmer as well. The highly modular and structured code we supply should be translatable into other forms of BASIC with a minimum of fuss and bother. Even if you write in COBOL on an IBM 370/168, you can use these subroutines by translating them into that language. The process of translation from BASIC to COBOL is after all quite simple for a COBOL programmer, compared to that programmer translating from COBOL to BASIC.

Most microcomputer vendors, IBM, Commodore, Radio Shack to name a few, use a common form of enhanced BASIC made by the Microsoft Company of Bellevue, Washington. If you have that kind of BASIC, you can copy any one of these programs and be pretty well assured that it will run on your machine. Some microcomputers, notably the APPLE-II, have a modified version of Microsoft BASIC, or use a different BASIC altogether.

If you have an APPLE-II and you see this program structure in this book:

```
ln-1  IF cond
        THEN st-1: st-2: st-3
        ELSE st-4: st-5: st-6
```

you can write it in APPLESOFT this way:

```
ln-1  IF cond THEN st-1: st-2: st-3: GOTO ln-3
ln-2  st-4: st-5: st-6
ln-3  .....
```

Aside from this difference in program structure, the enhanced BASIC on the TRS-80 and that on the APPLE-II are very similar for the purpose of running these programs.

The configuration we used when we wrote these subroutines was a TRS-80 Model III with LEVEL III BASIC, 48 K bytes of memory, and dual disks. In all cases, these subroutines will also run on a disk-system Model I or Model II, or on a TRS-80 color computer. A few of the programs use Disk BASIC features, and these are appropriately annotated. More about these features when we discuss programming standards later.

Subroutines Section Format

The layout of this book is unlike most others. Its intent is to serve as a reference volume, an assortment of program modules. Each module is presented within a four-page section. There are 36 such four-page modules, each of which is also carefully formatted, as explained below:

First page of each four-page module, always on the left.

NAME:

A single short phrase that uniquely identifies the subroutine.

PURPOSE:

A short phrase that tells what the subroutine does. This brief description if followed by one or two small paragraphs that explain in more detail what the subroutine does, how it can be used, and possibly some examples of input and output.

REFERENCE:

One or more useful citations (if available) where you can get more information.

SUBROUTINE LISTING:

The code, always starting at Line #1000 as a remark.

Second page of each four-page module:

VARIABLES:

An itemized listing of all variables. The entering variables are those that are passed from the main program to the subroutine. The exiting variables are the results that are passed back to the calling program. Last in this list are the local variables that the subroutine uses.

NOTES:

If other subroutines are called, they are cross-referenced. If there are restrictions or problems, such as the return of an integer or the alteration of an entering variable, they are discussed here. If there are special features, such as unexpected applications, they are mentioned.

Third page of each four-page module:

PROGRAM LISTING:

A single application that acts as a driver program that uses this subroutine. Note that the subroutine is listed within this program, so that you can refer conveniently to the next page with its discussion of output to see what the subroutine does.

OUTPUT:

A sample output as produced by the program above.

Last page of each four-page module:

OUTPUT (CONTINUED):

A continuation of the output, if necessary.

Mother Programs

Included in Part III of the book are five larger programs so that you can see some of these subroutines in the context of problem solving. These programs are substantially larger than the programs in Part II, and they incorporate several subroutines each. They represent actual applications rather than the smaller programs that are used to drive the subroutines in the second part of the book.

We expect most of you to become familiar with this chapter and the next, which explains in more detail how to use the subroutines, at a casual pace and in orderly sequential fashion. It is in Parts II and III that you will choose to use the various chapters in order of need.

CHAPTER

2

HOW TO USE THE SUBROUTINES

We have purposely designed a standardized four-page format for each subroutine to make these subroutines easy for you to use. You will find the same type of data and information at each location within the four pages. If you are looking for a specific area of discussion for a given subroutine, you will quickly learn to approximate where it is within the four pages.

Since each subroutine is generally quite short and always starts at line number 1000, it is a simple matter to copy it into an appropriate place in your own program. For example, if you have a program that needs to change a base 16, or hexadecimal, value to decimal, then you'll need Subroutine MA2. If you have lines 1000 to 1070 free, your task is simply to copy that subroutine directly; otherwise, you'll have to change the line numbers and write the subroutine into your code with different line numbers, say 3000 to 3070.

Once the subroutine is in place, you can use it by noting the entering and exiting variables. For example, MA2's entering variable is N$, a string representation of the hexadecimal number to be converted, and the exiting variable is D, the decimal equivalent of the entering string. Suppose you have inserted the subroutine at lines 7000-7070, and at line 350 of the main program you need to change the string X$, representing a hexadecimal number, into the numeric variable X, representing its decimal equivalent. Your main program would look like this:

```
            .
            .
    350 N$=X$: GOSUB 7000    ' <<<< call  .....
    360 X=D
            .
            .
```

If at line 740 you have to change B$—let's say B$ is the hexadecimal string "5EF8"—to a string representation of its decimal equivalent called X$, you could do it this way:

```
            .
            .
    740 N$=B$
    750 GOSUB 7000    ' <<<< call .....
    760 X$=STR$(D)
            .
            .
```

Programming Standards

We have tried diligently to exhibit the kinds of programming standards we would hope to find in programs we might need to modify at some future time. We have made both the subroutine and the driver program as readable as possible. They are modular in structure and are as free of GOTOs as reasonable.

Internal Documentation

All subroutines start at line numbers that are multiples of 1000. The subroutine under consideration starts at line 1000, which is always a remark. Spacing in the form of indentation and line feeds without carriage returns, such as

```
    1110 IF A = B
              THEN L = L + 1
              ELSE J = J - 1
```

maintain the high readability of every IF test. Multiple statement lines are allowed, but limited to only a few statements per line. This greatly reduces confusion on the part of the program's reader. FOR-NEXT loop bodies are always indented. Key instructions, such as the FOR, NEXT, GOSUB and RETURN, are always alone on a line, except for REMs where useful. All REMs use the TRS-80 (and otherwise popular) apostrophe instead of the characters REM. For example,

```
1120 GOSUB 2000        ' <<<< call timer
```

Output

In order to maximize accuracy, we have used actual computer output to exemplify all subroutines. The output has been kept Spartan in form. It shows that the subroutine works and what it produces, but it does not necessarily "prettify" results. It's up to you to round a result to whatever decimal position you desire, and to otherwise embellish the output.

Special Considerations

Because our hardware and software system has the MID$ function to the left of the assignment (=) symbol and the INSTR function, we use these functions when appropriate.

When the MID$ function appears on the right side of the = sign, which is its usual position in an expression, it is an extraction function. For example, the statement:

```
1590 A$=MID$(B$,M,N)
```

extracts from B$ the N characters starting at position M and places them in A$.

The MID$ function can appear on the left side of the = sign in IBM, Radio Shack, and Commodore BASIC programs, but not in APPLESOFT BASIC. For example, the statement:

```
1590 MID$(A$,M,N)=B$
```

is a replacement function. It replaces the N characters in A$ starting at position M with the string B$.

The INSTR function searches a string for the occurrence of a series of characters. In the statement:

```
1950 A=INSTR(B,X$,Y$)
```

the string X$ is searched starting at position B to see if the string Y$ occurs in it. If it does, the position of Y$ in X$ is returned in A. If Y$ is not found in X$, A is assigned the value 0.

For example, suppose V$ is the character string

PALANQUINISM AMONG TROBRIANDERS

and this statement is executed:

```
1950 L=INSTR(13,V$,"M")
```

The first occurrence of M in V$ is the last letter of PALANQUINISM, which is the 12th character. However, because the INSTR function stipulates the search to begin at the 13th character, the value 15 is placed in L, since the M in AMONG occurs as the 15th character of V$.

If your system configuration does not support the INSTR and MID$ to the left of the = sign, you can rewrite these sections of code. For example, if the line in More Subroutine Sandwich is

```
1750 MID$(X$,J,3) = LEFT$(Y$,N)
```

you can rewrite it as

```
1750 X$=LEFT$(X$,J-1)+LEFT$(Y$,N)+MID$(X$,J+3)
```

Suppose you find a line like this:

```
1800 R = INSTR(S,X$,"?")
```

Rewrite it as a loop, like this:

```
1800 FOR I = S TO LEN(X$)
1810   IF MID$(X$,I,1) = "?"
          THEN R = I: GOTO 1840
1820 NEXT I
1830 R = 0
1840 .....
```

Sample Program

Problem Statement

We have devoted this part of the introduction to a working sample of a mother program that incorporates three subroutines. The purpose of this application is to perform a statistical analysis on the frequency of word sizes in text. The overall structure of this program is, in hierarchical form:

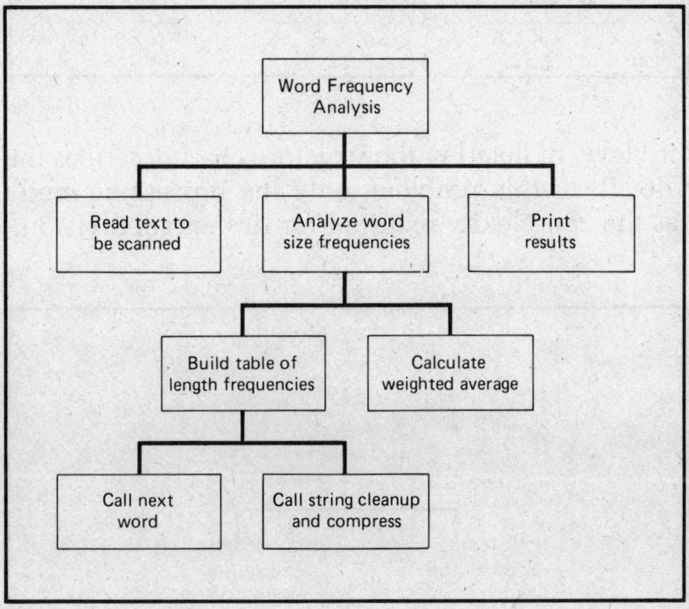

The structure chart has several features that tend to clarify the organization of this program. In general, all structure charts, like organization charts in a business, display the top-down ordering of the whole. The first block:

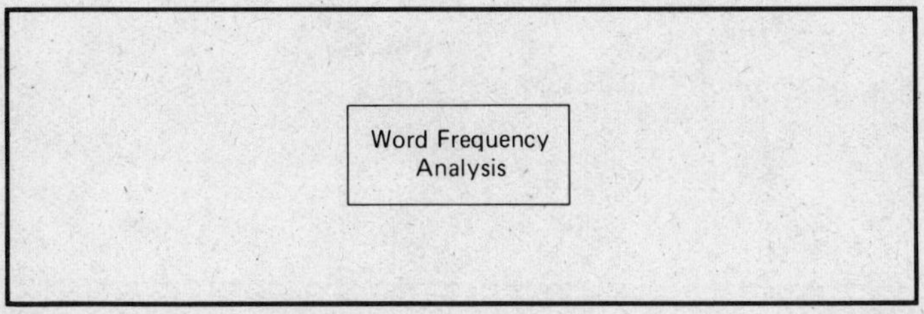

identifies the purpose of the entire program.

The second level of detail is divided into only three (input, processing, output) modules, because in this case the problem does not deal with storage in the form of files.

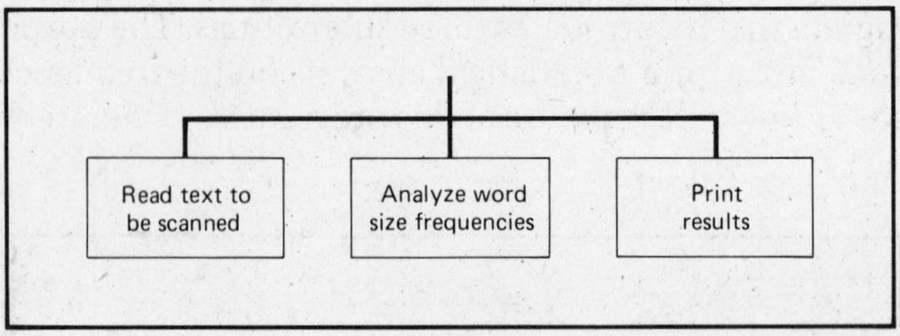

The third level of detail in the structure chart describes the problem in further detail. In this problem, only the processing module of the program has the complexity required for further subdivision.

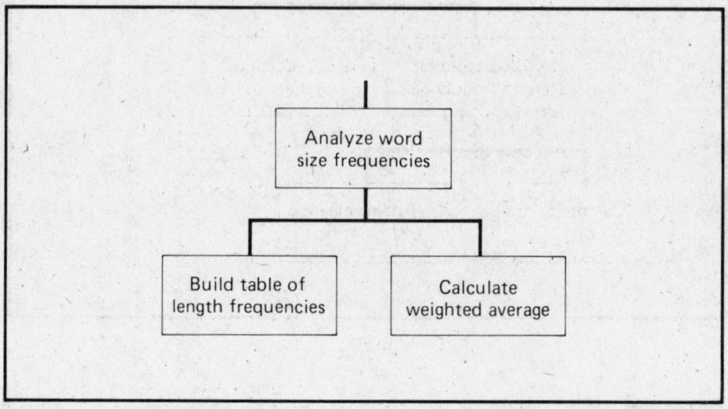

This problem has a fourth level of detail, describing the modular makeup of one of the third-level functions.

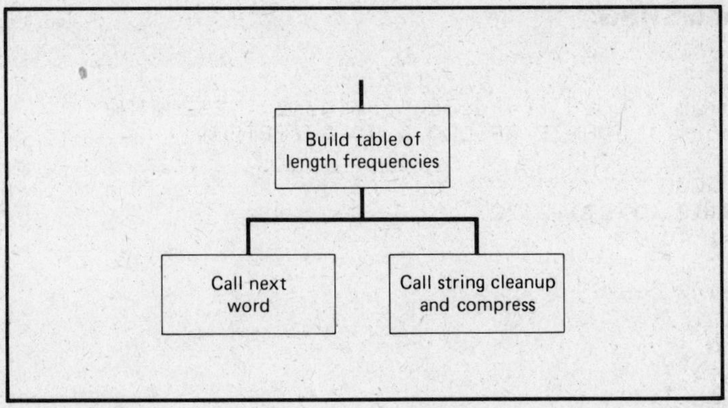

These last two modules are at the level of subroutines, which in the program are distinctly separate from the rest of the code.

CODE

Listed below are the entire calling program, its three embedded subroutines, and one sample of the program's output.

PROGRAM LISTING:

```
10 ' program : word frequency analysis : SS2MOTH0
20 ' authors : JOHN P GRILLO & JD ROBERTSON
30 '
40 CLEAR 2000
50 DIM T$(10),X(20),W(20)
60 FOR I=1 TO 20
70    X(I)=I
80    W(I)=0
90 NEXT I
100 READ N
110 FOR I=1 TO N
120    READ T$(I)
130 NEXT I
140 T$(N)=T$(N)+" #"
150 PRINT "words in text" : PRINT
160 V$=" abcdefghijklmnopqrstuvwxyz0123456789"
170 V$=V$+"ABCDEFGHIJKLMNOPQRSTUVWXYZ"
180 G=0 : K=1 : T=1
190 GOSUB 1000    ' <<<< call next word
200 IF G=1 THEN 280
210 S$=W$
220 GOSUB 3000    ' <<<< call string clean-up & compress
230 W$=S$
240 PRINT W$,
250 J=LEN(W$)
260 W(J)=W(J)+1
270 GOTO 190
280 PRINT : CLS
290 P$="  ##       ###                ##       ###"
300 PRINT "length  frequency          length  frequency"
310 FOR I=1 TO 20 STEP 2
320    PRINT USING P$;I,W(I),I+1,W(I+1)
330 NEXT I
340 GOSUB 2000   ' <<<< call weighted average
350 PRINT
360 PRINT "average word length";A
370 STOP
```

PROGRAM LISTING (CONTINUED):

```
380 DATA 7 :    ' okra
390 DATA "Okra can be grown in a sunny area where days and"
400 DATA "nights are warm.  Pods add body and flavor when"
410 DATA "cut up in soups, stews, catsup, and relishes."
420 DATA "Also delicious as a cooked vegetable.  Pick"
430 DATA "every two or three days for a continuous harvest."
440 DATA "Pods are best when young and small.  A packet of"
450 DATA "seeds will sow 15 ft. of row; one oz., 50 ft."
1000 ' **** next word
1010 W$=""
1020 IF G=1 THEN RETURN
1030 FOR I8=T TO LEN(T$(K))
1040     M8$=MID$(T$(K),I8,1)
1050     IF M8$="#" THEN G=1 : RETURN
1060     IF M8$<>" " THEN 1100
1070 NEXT I8
1080 K=K+1 : T=1
1090 IF W$=""
       THEN 1030
       ELSE G=0 : RETURN
1100 W$=W$+M8$
1110 IF I8=LEN(T$(K))
       THEN K=K+1 : T=1 :
            G=0 : RETURN
1120 FOR J8=I8+1 TO LEN(T$(K))
1130     M8$=MID$(T$(K),J8,1)
1140     IF M8$=" " THEN T=J8 : GOTO 1180
1150     W$=W$+M8$
1160 NEXT J8
1170 K=K+1 : T=1
1180 G=0
1190 RETURN
```

PROGRAM LISTING (CONTINUED):

```
2000 ' **** weighted average
2010 S8=0 : W8=0
2020 FOR I8=1 TO N
2030    S8=S8+W(I8)*X(I8)
2040    W8=W8+W(I8)
2050 NEXT I8
2060 A=S8/W8
2070 RETURN
3000 ' **** string clean-up & compress
3010 S8$=""
3020 FOR I8=1 TO LEN(S$)
3030    IF INSTR(V$,MID$(S$,I8,1))<>0
          THEN S8$=S8$+MID$(S$,I8,1)
3040 NEXT I8
3050 S$=S8$
3060 RETURN
9999 END
```

PROGRAM OUTPUT:

```
words in text

Okra           can            be             grown
in             a              sunny          area
where          days           and            nights
are            warm           Pods           add
body           and            flavor         when
cut            up             in             soups
stews          catsup         and            relishes
Also           delicious      as             a
cooked         vegetable      Pick           every
two            or             three          days
for            a              continuous     harvest
Pods           are            best           when
young          and            small          A
packet         of             seeds          will
sow            15             ft             of
row            one            oz             50
ft
length  frequency           length  frequency
   1        4                  2        13
   3       14                  4        14
   5       10                  6         5
   7        1                  8         1
   9        2                 10         1
  11        0                 12         0
  13        0                 14         0
  15        0                 16         0
  17        0                 18         0
  19        0                 20         0

average word length 3.52459
```

PROGRAM NOTES:

The program uses data stored in DATA statements in lines 390 through 450. With minor changes the program could input text from the keyboard or from a disk or tape file.

Lines 40 through 90 clear sufficient string space and initialize the two arrays, X for weights and W for word frequencies.

Lines 100 through 130 transfer the data strings to the array T$.

Line 140 forces the character pair _# (space and number symbol) at the end of the text as a terminator.

The loop consisting of lines 190 throught 270 fills the W array with word frequencies.

Lines 280 through 330 print the chart of word frequencies. This program uses the word frequencies as weights to compute the weighted average, and coincidentally uses the word lengths as subscripts for the frequency counter array W.

Lines 340 through 360 finish off the program's work, first calling the weighted average subroutine, then printing the result.

Conclusion

This chapter has outlined the programming practices we use in the subroutines. It has demonstrated how you can modify our code to your purposes, either if you have a different BASIC or if you need to call a subroutine from several places in the program. The brief discussion on MID$ and INSTR should help you to convert our statements that use these functions into your brand of the language if they are not available to you. We showed you a complete decomposition of a program, from problem statement through its structure and code to its output in order to exemplify the use of subroutines. With your understanding of these two introductory chapters you should be able to digest the meaty morsels in the middle of the sandwich.

As constant users of many of these subroutines, we can vouch for their accuracy, efficiency, speed, power, and most particularly, their ease of use. We are aware, of course, that this list of subroutines is not exhaustive. New ones will be continually developed and old ones improved.

We hope that you will enjoy these compact, powerful pieces of programming, and that you will discover some new and effective way to program your application. Remember that it will always be your recognition of a user's needs, rather than clever codes, that will mark you as a good programmer.

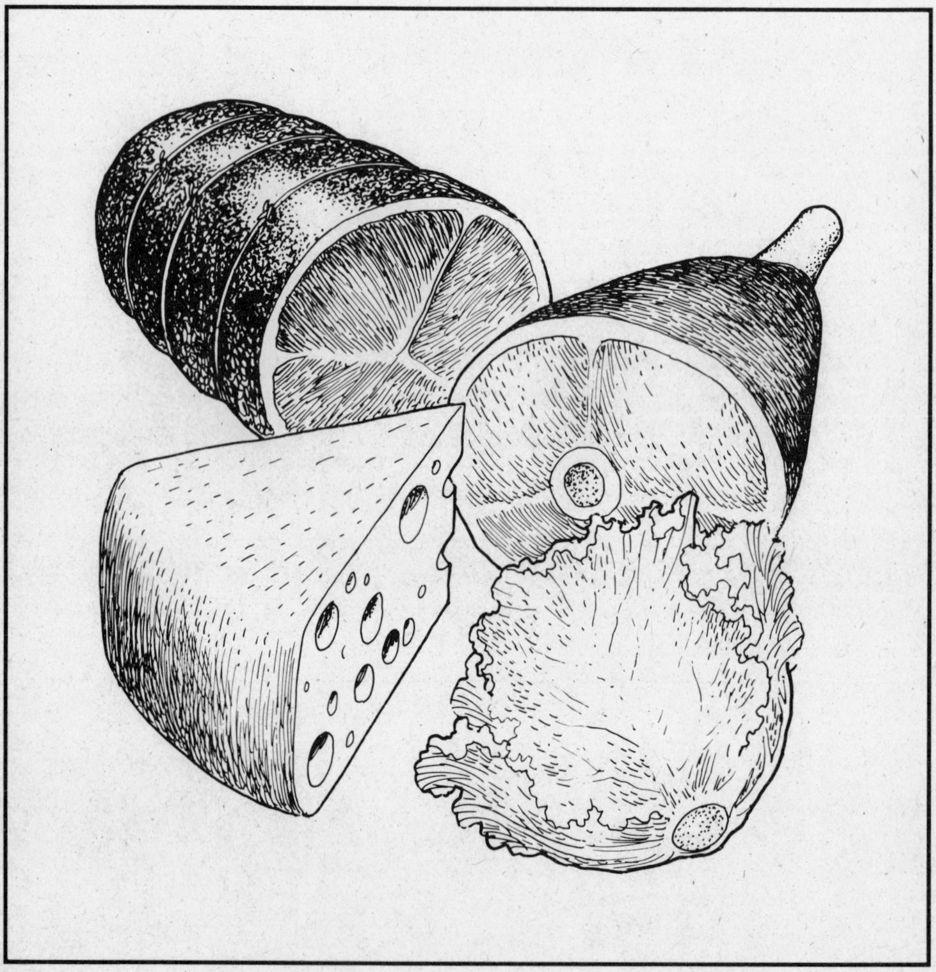

PART

II

Subroutines

Introduction

Chapters 3 through 10 that follow contain the substance of this book. Each chapter consists of three to nine subroutines that relate to each other. For example, Chapter 3, Date Processing, incorporates three subroutines that deal with Julian date calculations and day-of-the-year calculations. Chapter 8, Statistics, contains nine subroutines that would be useful in statistical applications. Our past experience with these subroutines has indicated that often the use of one subroutine leads to the use of another and that the second is closely related to the first. It is for this reason that we have grouped these subroutines according to their area of application.

CHAPTER

3

DATE PROCESSING

Introduction

The three subroutines that follow all deal with dates of the calendar. Typical areas of application are in programs that age accounts in an accounts receivable system, the generation of follow-up notices 30, 60, and 90 days after a bill is due, or simply the calculation of days between two dates for any reason. Tickler file programs, those that act as reminders to the user that this or that should be done today or tomorrow or next week, could use one or more of these subroutines. If you want to print a special calendar for someone, you need these subroutines.

Some of the date processing subroutines use the number 1721119 as a constant to provide a relative point in time from which to calculate all dates. That number, if entered as a Julian date in the Reverse Day of the Year subroutine DP3, yields the date February 29, year 0. The originators of that algorithm elected to use the first leap day of that millenium as a starting point.

Subroutine: Julian Date SS2DP1

PURPOSE:

Convert a month-day-year date to a unique number.

This subroutine converts a calendar date in month, day of month, and year form to a unique 7-digit number. Two consecutive calendar dates yield consecutive 7-digit numbers. Leap years and monthly boundaries are handled automatically. For example: October 9, 1980 is month 10, day 9, year 1980. The subroutine calculates the 7-digit number 2444522. The next day, October 10, 1980, yields the 7-digit number 2444523.

This subroutine is usable in any application that needs to know the number of days between two dates, particularly when those two dates are in different years. If the two dates fall within the same year, one could use SS1DP2, the Day of Year subroutine in Subroutine Sandwich Volume 1.

REFERENCE:

J. D. Robertson, "Remark on Algorithm 398," *Communications of the ACM,* Vol. 15, No. 10, 1972, p. 918.

LISTING:

```
1000 ' **** Julian date
1010  IF J>2
        THEN M8=J-3 : Y8=I
        ELSE M8=J+9 : Y8=I-1
1020  C8=INT(Y8/100) : D8=Y8-100*C8
1030  N#=INT(146097*C8/4)+K+INT(1461*D8/4)+1721119
           +INT((153*M8+2)/5)
1040 RETURN
```

VARIABLES:

```
entering

    I:  4-digit year. Example:  1982
    J:  1- or 2-digit month. Example:  1=Jan, 12=Dec
    K:  1- or 2-digit day of month.

exiting

    N#:  7-digit Julian date.

local

    C8: Century
    D8: Year in century
    M8: Adjusted month
    Y8: Adjusted year
```

NOTES:

N# is a double precision variable because the value returned by the subroutine is always a 7-digit number. Take care not to delete the constant 1721119 from line 1030 of the subroutine, even though it seems to be an arbitrary value that forces the answer into the 7-digit range. This value, and all other constants in that line, are crucial for the reverse Julian date subroutine SS2DP2, which follows.

This algorithm will return an accurate (relative to today) 7-digit Julian date back to October 24, 4713 B.C. Of course this is a bit ridiculous, since no Gregorian or Julian calendar existed back then. However, it is still noteworthy because the method takes into account the quadrennial leap years, the centennial non-leap years, the quadricentennial leap years, and even the millenial non-leap years.

PROGRAM LISTING:

```
10 ' program : Julian date : SS2DP1
20 ' authors : JOHN P GRILLO & JD ROBERTSON
30 '
40 PRINT
50 PRINT "input month, day, & year"
60 PRINT "  eg: 10,9,1982 means Oct 9, 1982"
70 INPUT J,K,I
80 IF J<=0 THEN STOP
90 GOSUB 1000     ' <<<< call Julian date
100 PRINT J;"/";K;"/";I;"--->";N#
110 GOTO 40
1000 ' **** Julian date
1010  IF J>2
        THEN M8=J-3 : Y8=I
        ELSE M8=J+9 : Y8=I-1
1020  C8=INT(Y8/100) : D8=Y8-100*C8
1030  N#=INT(146097*C8/4)+K+INT(1461*D8/4)+1721119
          +INT((153*M8+2)/5)
1040 RETURN
9999 END
```

RUN:

```
input month, day, & year
  eg: 10,9,1982 means Oct 9, 1982
? 6,13,1982
 6 / 13 / 1982 ---> 2445134

input month, day, & year
  eg: 10,9,1982 means Oct 9, 1982
? 1,1,1982
 1 / 1 / 1982 ---> 2444971

input month, day, & year
  eg: 10,9,1982 means Oct 9, 1982
? 1,1,1983
 1 / 1 / 1983 ---> 2445336

input month, day, & year
  eg: 10,9,1982 means Oct 9, 1982
? 10,9,1943
 10 / 9 / 1943 ---> 2431007

input month, day, & year
  eg: 10,9,1982 means Oct 9, 1982
? 9,10,1935
 9 / 10 / 1935 ---> 2428056
```

RUN (CONTINUED):

```
input month, day, & year
  eg: 10,9,1982 means Oct 9, 1982
? 2,27,1983
 2 / 27 / 1983 ---> 2445393

input month, day, & year
  eg: 10,9,1982 means Oct 9, 1982
? 2,28,1983
 2 / 28 / 1983 ---> 2445394

input month, day, & year
  eg: 10,9,1982 means Oct 9, 1982
? 3,1,1983
 3 / 1 / 1983 ---> 2445395

input month, day, & year
  eg: 10,9,1982 means Oct 9, 1982
? 3,2,1983
 3 / 2 / 1983 ---> 2445396

input month, day, & year
  eg: 10,9,1982 means Oct 9, 1982
? 2,27,1984
 2 / 27 / 1984 ---> 2445758

input month, day, & year
  eg: 10,9,1982 means Oct 9, 1982
? 2,28,1984
 2 / 28 / 1984 ---> 2445759

input month, day, & year
  eg: 10,9,1982 means Oct 9, 1982
? 2,29,1984
 2 / 29 / 1984 ---> 2445760

input month, day, & year
  eg: 10,9,1982 means Oct 9, 1982
? 3,1,1984
 3 / 1 / 1984 ---> 2445761

input month, day, & year
  eg: 10,9,1982 means Oct 9, 1982
? 3,2,1984
 3 / 2 / 1984 ---> 2445762
```

Subroutine: Reverse Julian Date SS2DP2

PURPOSE:

Convert a 7-digit Julian date to month-day-year format.

The previous algorithm changed a date in standard format to one in Julian format. This one reverses the procedure. It uses a 7-digit integer to produce a month-day-year date. Suppose you had to know the date that was exactly 100 days beyond Christmas day, 1935. First, you would call SS2DP1, the Julian date subroutine, entering 12,25,1935. The returned 7-digit Julian date, 2428162, plus 100 (now 2428262) is then given to this reversing subroutine. What you get back, 04/03/1936, is the date exactly 100 days after 12/25/1935. Even the fact that 1936 is a leap year is taken into consideration.

REFERENCE:

J. D. Robertson, "Remark on Algorithm 398," *Communications of the ACM*, Vol. 15, No. 10. 1972, p. 918.

LISTING:

```
1000 ' **** reverse Julian date
1010 M8=N#-1721119 : I=INT((4*M8-1)/146097)
1020 M8=4*M8-1-146097*I : K=INT(M8/4)
1030 M8=INT((4*K+3)/1461) : K=4*K+3-1461*M8
1040 K=INT((K+4)/4) : J=INT((5*K-3)/153)
1050 K=5*K-3-153*J : K=INT((K+5)/5)
1060 I=100*I+M8
1070 IF J<10
       THEN J=J+3
       ELSE J=J-9 : I=I+1
1080 RETURN
```

VARIABLES:

```
entering

   N#:  7-digit Julian date. Example, 24445123.

exiting

   I:  Year of Gregorian calendar.
   J:  Month of the year.
   K:  Day of the month.

local

   M8:  Intermediate value.
```

NOTES:

You may recognize the integer constants 1721119, 146097, 1461, and 153 from the Julian date subroutine. These values are essential for this reversing process to occur correctly.

In line 1010, the first action is to subtract 1721119 from the entered 7-digit Julian date. The variable M8 need not be double-precision because once you have reduced N# by 1721119, the amount left is no longer very large. However, if your Julian date entered is unusually far into the future, say beyond A.D. 5000, you should work solely with double precision variables.

PROGRAM LISTING:

```
10 ' program : reverse Julian date : SS2DP2
20 ' authors : JOHN P GRILLO & JD ROBERTSON
30 '
40 PRINT
50 PRINT "input Julian date 7-digit number"
60 PRINT "  eg: 2445001"
70 INPUT N#
80 IF N#<=0 THEN STOP
90 GOSUB 1000    ' <<<< call reverse Julian date
100 PRINT N#;"--->";J;"/";K;"/";I
110 GOTO 40
1000 ' **** reverse Julian date
1010 M8=N#-1721119 : I=INT((4*M8-1)/146097)
1020 M8=4*M8-1-146097*I : K=INT(M8/4)
1030 M8=INT((4*K+3)/1461) : K=4*K+3-1461*M8
1040 K=INT((K+4)/4) : J=INT((5*K-3)/153)
1050 K=5*K-3-153*J : K=INT((K+5)/5)
1060 I=100*I+M8
1070 IF J<10
       THEN J=J+3
       ELSE J=J-9 : I=I+1
1080 RETURN
9999 END
```

RUN:

```
input Julian date 7-digit number
  eg: 2445001
? 2445134
 2445134 ---> 6 / 13 / 1982

input Julian date 7-digit number
  eg: 2445001
? 2444971
 2444971 ---> 1 / 1 / 1982

input Julian date 7-digit number
  eg: 2445001
? 2445336
 2445336 ---> 1 / 1 / 1983

input Julian date 7-digit number
  eg: 2445001
? 2431007
 2431007 ---> 10 / 9 / 1943

input Julian date 7-digit number
  eg: 2445001
? 2428056
 2428056 ---> 9 / 10 / 1935
```

RUN (CONTINUED):

```
input Julian date 7-digit number
  eg: 2445001
? 2445393
 2445393 ---> 2 / 27 / 1983

input Julian date 7-digit number
  eg: 2445001
? 2445394
 2445394 ---> 2 / 28 / 1983

input Julian date 7-digit number
  eg: 2445001
? 2445395
 2445395 ---> 3 / 1 / 1983

input Julian date 7-digit number
  eg: 2445001
? 2445396
 2445396 ---> 3 / 2 / 1983

input Julian date 7-digit number
  eg: 2445001
? 2445758
 2445758 ---> 2 / 27 / 1984

input Julian date 7-digit number
  eg: 2445001
? 2445759
 2445759 ---> 2 / 28 / 1984

input Julian date 7-digit number
  eg: 2445001
? 2445760
 2445760 ---> 2 / 29 / 1984

input Julian date 7-digit number
  eg: 2445001
? 2445761
 2445761 ---> 3 / 1 / 1984

input Julian date 7-digit number
  eg: 2445001
? 2445762
 2445762 ---> 3 / 2 / 1984
```

Subroutine: Reverse Day of the Year SS2DP3

PURPOSE:

Convert a day of the year to a standard calendar date.

Here the point is to do the reverse of SS1DP2, the day-of-the-year subroutine in Subroutine Sandwich Volume 1. Instead of converting a date in month-day-year format to an integer from 1 to 366, this subroutine performs the reverse. You enter a 4-digit year and a day of year from 1 to 366, and you get back the month and day of the month.

REFERENCE:

J. D. Robertson, "Remark on Algorithm 398," *Communications of the ACM,* Vol. 15, No. 10, 1972, p. 918.

LISTING:

```
1000 ' **** reverse day of the year
1010 GOSUB 2000    ' <<<< call leap year
1020 IF N>59+L
       THEN K=N+2-L
       ELSE K=N
1030 J=INT(100*(K+91)/3055)
1040 K=K+91-INT(3055*J/100)
1050 J=J-2
1060 RETURN
```

VARIABLES:

```
entering

    I:  4-digit year.  Example:  1982
    N:  Day number within that year. Example:  220


exiting

    J:  Month number, from 1 to 12
    K:  Day of the month, from 1 to 31


local

    None
```

NOTES:

The instruction in line 1010 to call the leap year subroutine is necessary because the user must have the freedom to choose any year. If the user selects a leap year, the dates must be adjusted appropriately. Note that the leap year subroutine is described fully in the first book Subroutine Sandwich as SS1DP3.

In the calling program, line 100 is yet another use of a favorite technique to extract a portion of a string. J, the month number, is converted to a starting position for extraction. If J is 8, for example, 3*8-2 is 22, and the characters representing the 8th month, "AUG," start at the 22nd position in the string.

PROGRAM LISTING:

```
10 ' program : reverse day of the year : SS2DP3
20 ' authors : JOHN P GRILLO & JD ROBERTSON
30 '
40 PRINT
50 PRINT "input year and day of the year"
60 PRINT "  eg: 1982,282 means 282-nd day of year 1982"
70 INPUT I,N
80 IF I<=0 THEN STOP
90 GOSUB 1000    ' <<<< call reverse day of the year
100 M$=MID$("JANFEBMARAPRMAYJUNJULAUGSEPOCTNOVDEC",3*J-2,3)
110 PRINT "day";N;"of year";I;"is ";M$;K
120 GOTO 40
1000 ' **** reverse day of the year
1010 GOSUB 2000    ' <<<< call leap year
1020 IF N>59+L
       THEN K=N+2-L
       ELSE K=N
1030 J=INT(100*(K+91)/3055)
1040 K=K+91-INT(3055*J/100)
1050 J=J-2
1060 RETURN
2000 ' #### leap year
2010 L=0
2020 IF I=4*INT(I/4) THEN L=1
2030 IF I=100*INT(I/100) THEN L=0
2040 IF I=400*INT(I/400) THEN L=1
2050 RETURN
9999 END
```

RUN:

```
input year and day of the year
  eg: 1982,282 means 282-nd day of year 1982
? 1982,1
day 1 of year 1982 is JAN 1

input year and day of the year
  eg: 1982,282 means 282-nd day of year 1982
? 1982,365
day 365 of year 1982 is DEC 31
```

RUN (CONTINUED):

```
input year and day of the year
  eg: 1982,282 means 282-nd day of year 1982
? 1984,366
day 366 of year 1984 is DEC 31

input year and day of the year
  eg: 1982,282 means 282-nd day of year 1982
? 1982,58
day 58 of year 1982 is FEB 27

input year and day of the year
  eg: 1982,282 means 282-nd day of year 1982
? 1982,59
day 59 of year 1982 is FEB 28

input year and day of the year
  eg: 1982,282 means 282-nd day of year 1982
? 1982,60
day 60 of year 1982 is MAR 1

input year and day of the year
  eg: 1982,282 means 282-nd day of year 1982
? 1982,61
day 61 of year 1982 is MAR 2

input year and day of the year
  eg: 1982,282 means 282-nd day of year 1982
? 1984,58
day 58 of year 1984 is FEB 27

input year and day of the year
  eg: 1982,282 means 282-nd day of year 1982
? 1984,59
day 59 of year 1984 is FEB 28

input year and day of the year
  eg: 1982,282 means 282-nd day of year 1982
? 1984,60
day 60 of year 1984 is FEB 29

input year and day of the year
  eg: 1982,282 means 282-nd day of year 1982
? 1984,61
day 61 of year 1984 is MAR 1

input year and day of the year
  eg: 1982,282 means 282-nd day of year 1982
? 1984,62
day 62 of year 1984 is MAR 2
```

...HIJK
C
RNS
...-TWAS BRILLIG AND THE SLITHY TOVES...

CHAPTER

4

WORD PROCESSING

Introduction

Word processing as a discipline in applications programming has become highly popular recently because of its profitable use in the office environment. Instead of using typewriters and their attendant messy carbon copies, their problems of erasures, and their bothersome clackety noise, many offices today either have or are contemplating the purchase of word processors. These devices consist of a combination of computer hardware, editing programs, and a high-quality printer.

With a word processor, secretaries can generate letters with easily alterable addresses and contents. Mailing lists are more conveniently produced. Even the spelling of entered text can be checked with built-in dictionaries.

The convenience of working with the word processor has allowed a flexibility of format and text alteration that never existed before.

Each of the four subroutines that follow deals with some aspect of programming that is used in producing the word processing software so commonly found in today's offices.

Subroutine: String Cleanup and Compress SS2WP1

PURPOSE:

Remove special characters from a string.

A close cousin to this subroutine exists in Volume 1 of Subroutine Sandwich. That program is SS1WP1, our first string cleanup routine. The difference between the two is not in the special characters that each recognizes, but rather in what each subroutine does with those characters. SS1WP1 was designed to replace each special character with a blank. This subroutine squeezes out each special character, which results in a smaller string (unless, of course, no special characters were found).

The characters that are not touched are defined in the calling program as V$, so they are user dependent. In our example, the legal characters are the ten digits 0 to 9, the space, and the 26 lowercase letters of the alphabet.

REFERENCE:

Word processing references are scarce. We mention the words of caution concerning special characters in the SCRIPSIT manual for TRS-80 word processing. See also DecSystem10 "Getting Started With RUNOFF Text Formatting Program," DEC-10-URUNA-A-D (Digital Equipment Corporation, 1975).

LISTING:

```
1000 ' **** string clean-up & compress
1010 S8$=""
1020 FOR I8=1 TO LEN(S$)
1030     IF INSTR(V$,MID$(S$,I8,1))<>0
           THEN S8$=S8$+MID$(S$,I8,1)
1040 NEXT I8
1050 S$=S8$
1060 RETURN
```

VARIABLES:

```
entering

   S$:  String to be processed
   V$:  String of legal characters to be kept


exiting

   S$:  Cleaned string with no special characters


local

   S8$:  Temporary string buffer
   I8:   Loop index
```

NOTES:

The CLEAR instruction in line 40 is needed because of the way this subroutine works. S8$ increases in size during processing until it is in fact the returned string. Were this subroutine like the other cleanup subroutine in the previous volume, the special characters would have been replaced with a blank in place, with the MID$ function.

Line 1030 uses the INSTR to check for special characters. You may think of this line as "if the I8th character of S$ is in V$, attach it to S8$."

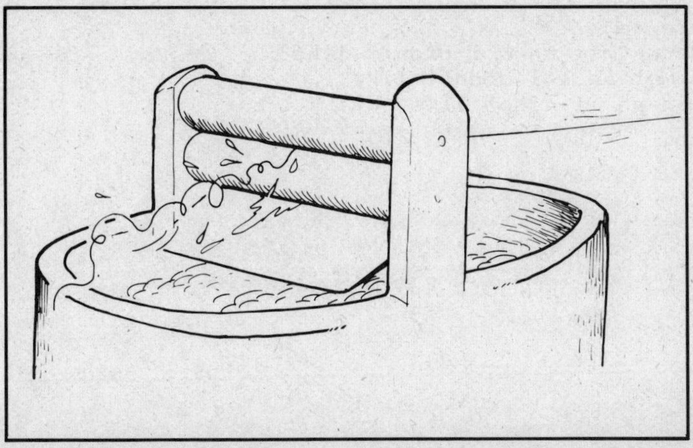

PROGRAM LISTING:

```
10 ' program : string clean-up & compress : SS2WP1
20 ' authors : JOHN P GRILLO & JD ROBERTSON
30 '
40 CLEAR 1000
50 PRINT
60 PRINT "input sentence"
70 PRINT "  eg: i never met an & i didn't like!"
80 INPUT S$
90 IF S$="" THEN STOP
100 V$="0123456789 abcdefghijklmnopqrstuvwxyz"
110 GOSUB 1000    ' <<<< call string clean-up & compress
120 PRINT S$
130 GOTO 50
1000 ' **** string clean-up & compress
1010 S8$=""
1020 FOR I8=1 TO LEN(S$)
1030     IF INSTR(V$,MID$(S$,I8,1))<>0
          THEN S8$=S8$+MID$(S$,I8,1)
1040 NEXT I8
1050 S$=S8$
1060 RETURN
9999 END
```

RUN:

```
input sentence
  eg: i never met an & i didn't like!
? "delete hyphens (-),ampersands (&), and their ilk."
delete hyphens  ampersands  and their ilk

input sentence
  eg: i never met an & i didn't like!
? i regret that i have but one * for my country
i regret that i have but one  for my country

input sentence
  eg: i never met an & i didn't like!
? i never met an & i didn't like!
i never met an  i didnt like
```

RUN (CONTINUED):

```
input sentence
  eg: i never met an & i didn't like!
? "lenny: tell me 'bout the rabbits, george!"
lenny tell me bout the rabbits george

input sentence
  eg: i never met an & i didn't like!
? good grief!  clams got feet?
good grief  clams got feet

input sentence
  eg: i never met an & i didn't like!
? m*a*s*his one of my fav'rite t.v. programs
mash is one of my favrite tv programs

input sentence
  eg: i never met an & i didn't like!
? parentheses are cheap (they admitted parenthetically)
parentheses are cheap they admitted parenthetically

input sentence
  eg: i never met an & i didn't like!
? moe&larry&curly
moelarrycurly

input sentence
  eg: i never met an & i didn't like!
? chico-groucho-harpo-zeppo-gummo-karl
chicogrouchoharpozeppogummokarl

input sentence
  eg: i never met an & i didn't like!
? 3 grooved ormthets 'under-knurled' @ 5.98/unit
3 grooved ormthets underknurled  598unit
```

Subroutine: Next Word SS2WP2

PURPOSE:

Obtain the next word in line from a list of phrases.

The subroutine is called "next word" because in effect it gets the next word in a phrase. This algorithm or a similar one is essential in most word processing programs in order to break up the text into its component parts.

REFERENCE:

This algorithm is our own home brew for text analysis.

LISTING:

```
1000 ' **** next word
1010 W$=""
1020 IF G=1 THEN RETURN
1030 FOR I8=T TO LEN(T$(K))
1040    M8$=MID$(T$(K),I8,1)
1050    IF M8$="#" THEN G=1 : RETURN
1060    IF M8$<>" " THEN 1100
1070 NEXT I8
1080 K=K+1 : T=1
1090 IF W$=""
      THEN 1030
      ELSE G=0 : RETURN
1100 W$=W$+M8$
1110 IF I8=LEN(T$(K))
      THEN K=K+1 : T=1 :
           G=0 : RETURN
1120 FOR J8=I8+1 TO LEN(T$(K))
1130    M8$=MID$(T$(K),J8,1)
1140    IF M8$=" " THEN T=J8 : GOTO 1180
1150    W$=W$+M8$
1160 NEXT J8
1170 K=K+1 : T=1
1180 G=0
1190 RETURN
```

VARIABLES:

```
    entering

       T$:   List of phrases to be broken up into words

    exiting

       W$:   Next word
       G:    Indicator for end of processing. As long
             as G=0, there is more text to be analyzed
       K:    Phrase pointer
       T:    Position in the phrase being analyzed

    local

       I8:   Loop index for phrase
       M8$:  Character being scanned
       J8:   Loop index for word
```

NOTES:

The calling program attaches the characters "_#" to the last phrase T$(N) in line 100. Then it initializes the indicators and pointers G, K, T, and J as necessary. The subroutine is called as long as G is 0. The subroutine checks for end-of-text ("#") or end-of-word (" ") first in lines 1030 to 1090. If it is in the middle of a word, the program resumes the scan in lines 1100 to 1190.

The calling program supplies the text as a list of phrases. It also must pass several flags to indicate the status of the text processing. The returned single word is made up of all nonblank characters up to the next blank. It is the calling program's job to place an end character after the last string.

PROGRAM LISTING:

```
10 ' program : next word : SS2WP2
20 ' authors : JOHN P GRILLO & JD ROBERTSON
30 '
40 CLEAR 2000
50 DIM T$(10)
60 READ N
70 FOR I=1 TO N
80    READ T$(I)
90 NEXT I
100 PRINT "text word by word"
110 T$(N)=T$(N)+" #"
120 G=0 : K=1 : T=1
130 J=0
140 GOSUB 1000    ' <<<< call next word
150 IF G=1 THEN 200
160 IF J=INT(J/4)*4 THEN PRINT
170 J=J+1
180 PRINT J;W$;"    ";
190 GOTO 140
200 STOP
210 DATA 7 :    ' okra
220 DATA "Okra can be grown in a sunny area where days and"
230 DATA "nights are warm.  Pods add body and flavor when"
240 DATA "cut up in soups, stews, catsup, and relishes."
250 DATA "Also delicious as a cooked vegetable.  Pick"
260 DATA "every two or three days for a continuous harvest."
270 DATA "Pods are best when young and small.  A packet of"
280 DATA "seeds will sow 15 ft. of row; one oz., 50 ft."
1000 ' **** next word
1010 W$=""
1020 IF G=1 THEN RETURN
1030 FOR I8=T TO LEN(T$(K))
1040    M8$=MID$(T$(K),I8,1)
1050    IF M8$="#" THEN G=1 : RETURN
1060    IF M8$<>" " THEN 1100
1070 NEXT I8
1080 K=K+1 : T=1
1090 IF W$=""
       THEN 1030
       ELSE G=0 : RETURN
```

PROGRAM LISTING (CONTINUED):

```
1100 W$=W$+M8$
1110 IF I8=LEN(T$(K))
       THEN K=K+1 : T=1 :
            G=0 : RETURN
1120 FOR J8=I8+1 TO LEN(T$(K))
1130    M8$=MID$(T$(K),J8,1)
1140    IF M8$=" " THEN T=J8 : GOTO 1180
1150    W$=W$+M8$
1160 NEXT J8
1170 K=K+1 : T=1
1180 G=0
1190 RETURN
9999 END
```

RUN:

```
text word by word

 1 Okra    2 can     3 be     4 grown
 5 in      6 a     7 sunny     8 area
 9 where     10 days     11 and     12 nights
 13 are     14 warm.     15 Pods     16 add
 17 body     18 and     19 flavor     20 when
 21 cut     22 up     23 in     24 soups,
 25 stews,     26 catsup,     27 and     28 relishes.
 29 Also     30 delicious     31 as     32 a
 33 cooked     34 vegetable.     35 Pick     36 every
 37 two     38 or     39 three     40 days
 41 for     42 a     43 continuous     44 harvest.
 45 Pods     46 are     47 best     48 when
 49 young     50 and     51 small.     52 A
 53 packet     54 of     55 seeds     56 will
 57 sow     58 15     59 ft.     60 of
 61 row;     62 one     63 oz.,     64 50
 65 ft.
Break in 200
READY
>
```

Subroutine: Buffer Fill SS2WP3

PURPOSE:

Produce a line of text within given margins.

Once you have broken up a set of text into its component words, the next task is to fit into a given line of fixed length as many words as possible. The line of fixed length that the calling program supplies is called a buffer, and the subroutine's task is to fill that buffer.

The calling program is very similar to the previous one, which called the "next word" subroutine. In this one, however, one additional parameter must be passed, and that is the width of the buffer.

REFERENCE:

DecSystem10 "Getting Started With RUNOFF Text Formatting Program," DEC-10-URUNA-A-D (Digital Equipment Corporation, 1975), p. 11. Quoting from this source, ".FILL adds successive words from the source text until the adding of one more word will exceed the right margin." The RUNOFF word processing system has been emulated by several vendors, notably PRIME. You may wish to consult these manuals. Also, note that this subroutine is much like the WINDOW command in Radio Shack's SCRIPSIT word processor.

LISTING:

```
1000 ' **** buffer fill
1010 B$=""
1020 IF W$=""
     THEN GOSUB 2000    ' <<<< call next word
1030 IF G=1 THEN RETURN
1040 IF LEN(B$)+LEN(W$)<=W-1
     THEN B$=B$+W$+" " : W$="" : GOTO 1020
1050 IF RIGHT$(B$,1)=" " THEN B$=LEFT$(B$,LEN(B$)-1)
1060 RETURN
```

VARIABLES:

```
entering

    T$:      List of text strings
    W:       Buffer width
    G:       Indicator for next word subroutine

exiting

    B$:      Filled buffer

local

    None.  However, note that the next word subroutine
       uses several
```

NOTES:

The buffer fill subroutine must call the next word subroutine for its input. As long as the indicator G is 0, the next word subroutine is called for more words. Each word is concatenated, or attached, to the list of words in B$ as long as the length of B$ doesn't exceed the buffer width. When the next word is too large to fit in B$, it is used as the first word in the next B$ buffer.

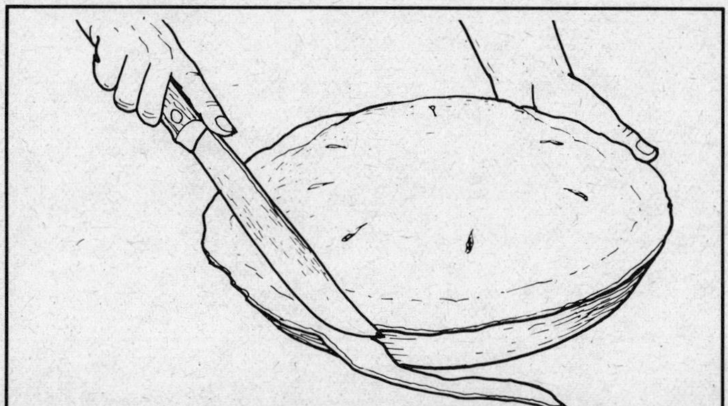

PROGRAM LISTING:

```
10 ' program : buffer fill : SS2WP3
20 ' authors : JOHN P GRILLO & JD ROBERTSON
30 '
40 CLEAR 2000
50 DIM T$(10)
60 READ N
70 FOR I=1 TO N
80    READ T$(I)
90 NEXT I
100 T$(N)=T$(N)+" #"
110 G=0 : K=1 : T=1
120 INPUT "input buffer width";W : PRINT
130 PRINT "text in";W;"character buffers" : PRINT
140 J=0
150 GOSUB 1000    ' <<<< call buffer fill
160 J=J+1
170 PRINT J;TAB(10);B$
180 IF G=1 THEN STOP
190 GOTO 150
200 STOP
210 DATA 7 :    ' okra
220 DATA "Okra can be grown in a sunny area where days and"
230 DATA "nights are warm.  Pods add body and flavor when"
240 DATA "cut up in soups, stews, catsup, and relishes."
250 DATA "Also delicious as a cooked vegetable.  Pick"
260 DATA "every two or three days for a continuous harvest."
270 DATA "Pods are best when young and small.  A packet of"
280 DATA "seeds will sow 15 ft. of row; one oz., 50 ft."
1000 ' **** buffer fill
1010 B$=""
1020 IF W$=""
       THEN GOSUB 2000    ' <<<< call next word
1030 IF G=1 THEN RETURN
1040 IF LEN(B$)+LEN(W$)<=W-1
       THEN B$=B$+W$+" " : W$="" : GOTO 1020
1050 IF RIGHT$(B$,1)=" " THEN B$=LEFT$(B$,LEN(B$)-1)
1060 RETURN
```

PROGRAM LISTING (CONTINUED):

```
2000 ' #### next word
2010 W$=""
2020 IF G=1 THEN RETURN
2030 FOR I8=T TO LEN(T$(K))
2040    M8$=MID$(T$(K),I8,1)
2050    IF M8$="#" THEN G=1 : RETURN
2060    IF M8$<>" " THEN 2100
2070 NEXT I8
2080 K=K+1 : T=1
2090 IF W$=""
       THEN 2030
       ELSE G=0 : RETURN
2100 W$=W$+M8$
2110 IF I8=LEN(T$(K))
       THEN K=K+1 : T=1 :
            G=0 : RETURN
2120 FOR J8=I8+1 TO LEN(T$(K))
2130    M8$=MID$(T$(K),J8,1)
2140    IF M8$=" " THEN T=J8 : GOTO 2180
2150    W$=W$+M8$
2160 NEXT J8
2170 K=K+1 : T=1
2180 G=0
2190 RETURN
9999 END
```

RUN:

```
input buffer width? 30

text in 30 character buffers

 1        Okra can be grown in a sunny
 2        area where days and nights
 3        are warm. Pods add body and
 4        flavor when cut up in soups,
 5        stews, catsup, and relishes.
 6        Also delicious as a cooked
 7        vegetable. Pick every two or
 8        three days for a continuous
 9        harvest. Pods are best when
 10       young and small. A packet of
 11       seeds will sow 15 ft. of row;
 12       one oz., 50 ft.
```

Subroutine: Text Justify SS2WP4

PURPOSE:

Justify a line of text in a buffer.

As a final step in word processing after breaking up the text into words and filling a buffer of given length with as many words as possible, you should have a way to justify the text. This means inserting however many blanks are necessary between the words to make the rightmost word end at the right margin.

REFERENCE:

The several forms of RUNOFF all have a .JUSTIFY command that does the same thing as this subroutine. Radio Shack's SCRIPSIT has a formatting command, J=Y, which justifies the text string.

LISTING:

```
1000 ' **** text justify
1010 RANDOM
1020 N8=W-LEN(B$)
1030 IF N8=0 THEN RETURN
1040 IF L=1 THEN B$=B$+STRING$(W-LEN(B$)," ") : RETURN
1050 IF INSTR(B$," ")=0 THEN B$=B$+" "
1060 J8=1
1070 FOR I8=1 TO N8
1080    J8=INSTR(J8,B$," ")
1090    IF J8=0 THEN J8=RND(LEN(B$)) : GOTO 1080
1100    IF RND(2)>1
          THEN B$=LEFT$(B$,J8)+" "+RIGHT$(B$,LEN(B$)-J8)
          ELSE J8=J8+1 : GOTO 1080
1110    J8=J8+2
1120 NEXT I8
1130 RETURN
```

VARIABLES:

```
entering

    B$:  Buffer, filled with words
    W:   Width of buffer
    L:   Last buffer indicator


exiting

    B$:  Buffer, with right-justified text


local

    N8:  Number of blanks to be inserted
    J8:  Position of next blank between words in B$
    I8:  Loop index
```

NOTES:

Several features highlight this subroutine. Notice that lines 1080 and 1090 work together to find a blank between words that is randomly positioned rather than being the next available blank space. Line 1100 also uses the RND function, only this time it is used to place the blank between the words only half the time. The overall effect of these two routines working together is to produce text strings with the spacing between words distributed to yield highly readable text.

As in the two previous subroutines, which are both called by this one, the calling routine must supply several items of information, including buffer width, text phrases, and initialized indicators. In return, the subroutine will produce a text string that ends precisely on the right margin.

PROGRAM LISTING:

```
10 ' program : text justify : SS2WP4
20 ' authors : JOHN P GRILLO & JD ROBERTSON
30 '
40 CLEAR 2000
50 DIM T$(10)
60 READ N
70 FOR I=1 TO N
80    READ T$(I)
90 NEXT I
100 T$(N)=T$(N)+" #"
110 G=0 : K=1 : T=1
120 INPUT "input buffer width";W : PRINT
130 PRINT "text justified in";W;"character buffers" : PRINT
140 J=0
150 GOSUB 2000  ' <<<< call buffer fill
160 IF G=1 THEN L=1
170 J=J+1
180 GOSUB 1000   ' <<<< call text justify
190 PRINT J;TAB(10);B$
200 IF G=1 THEN STOP
210 GOTO 150
220 STOP
230 DATA 7 :    ' okra
240 DATA "Okra can be grown in a sunny area where days and"
250 DATA "nights are warm.  Pods add body and flavor when"
260 DATA "cut up in soups, stews, catsup, and relishes."
270 DATA "Also delicious as a cooked vegetable.  Pick"
280 DATA "every two or three days for a continuous harvest."
290 DATA "Pods are best when young and small.  A packet of"
300 DATA "seeds will sow 15 ft. of row; one oz., 50 ft."
1000 ' **** text justify
1010 RANDOM
1020 N8=W-LEN(B$)
1030 IF N8=0 THEN RETURN
1040 IF L=1 THEN B$=B$+STRING$(W-LEN(B$)," ") : RETURN
1050 IF INSTR(B$," ")=0 THEN B$=B$+" "
1060 J8=1
1070 FOR I8=1 TO N8
1080    J8=INSTR(J8,B$," ")
1090    IF J8=0 THEN J8=RND(LEN(B$)) : GOTO 1080
1100    IF RND(2)>1
          THEN B$=LEFT$(B$,J8)+" "+RIGHT$(B$,LEN(B$)-J8)
          ELSE J8=J8+1 : GOTO 1080
1110    J8=J8+2
1120 NEXT I8
1130 RETURN
```

PROGRAM LISTING (CONTINUED):

```
2000 ' **** buffer fill
2010 B$=""
2020 IF W$=""
       THEN GOSUB 3000     ' <<<< call next word
2030 IF G=1 THEN RETURN
2040 IF LEN(B$)+LEN(W$)<=W-1
       THEN B$=B$+W$+" " : W$="" : GOTO 2020
2050 IF RIGHT$(B$,1)=" " THEN B$=LEFT$(B$,LEN(B$)-1)
2060 RETURN
3000 ' #### next word
3010 W$=""
3020 IF G=1 THEN RETURN
3030 FOR I8=T TO LEN(T$(K))
3040    M8$=MID$(T$(K),I8,1)
3050    IF M8$="#" THEN G=1 : RETURN
3060    IF M8$<>" " THEN 3100
3070 NEXT I8
3080 K=K+1 : T=1
3090 IF W$=""
       THEN 3030
       ELSE G=0 : RETURN
3100 W$=W$+M8$
3110 IF I8=LEN(T$(K))
       THEN K=K+1 : T=1 :
            G=0 : RETURN
3120 FOR J8=I8+1 TO LEN(T$(K))
3130    M8$=MID$(T$(K),J8,1)
3140    IF M8$=" " THEN T=J8 : GOTO 3180
3150    W$=W$+M8$
3160 NEXT J8
3170 K=K+1 : T=1
3180 G=0
3190 RETURN
9999 END
```

RUN:

```
input buffer width? 30

text justified in 30 character buffers

 1        Okra can  be grown in  a sunny
 2        area where  days  and  nights
 3        are  warm.  Pods  add body and
 4        flavor when cut  up  in soups,
 5        stews, catsup,  and  relishes.
 6        Also delicious as  a   cooked
 7        vegetable.  Pick every  two or
 8        three  days for  a  continuous
 9        harvest. Pods   are best  when
 10       young  and  small. A packet of
 11       seeds  will sow 15 ft. of row;
 12       one oz., 50 ft.
```

ABSOLUTELY SECRET
EVEN MORE SECRET
ULTRA
DO NOT READ
TOP SECRET
CONFIDENTIAL
EYES ONLY
MOST SECRET

CHAPTER

5

CRYPTOGRAPHY

Introduction

The symbols we use for this general class of subroutines—CR1, CR2, CR3—stand for the word "cryptography." This does not mean that you could market these programs to some clandestine spy organizations. We use the word in its more general form, to indicate the transformation of readable text into a set of characters that hide (as in a crypt, hence cryptic) the meaning of the original text. Therefore you could consider the process of encryption to be that of "burying" your text out of sight, but mostly out of easy comprehension.

Many applications for these techniques exist. You can password-protect program and data files in coded form; you can transmit messages over public phones; you can code messages to your friends; you can produce cryptograms; you can simply enjoy the challenge of trying to decode someone else's efforts.

Subroutine: Cyclic Prime Code SS2CR1

PURPOSE:

Encode and decode text by cyclic selection of letter positions.

One of the difficulties with simple substitution codes is that these codes can be broken with a frequency analysis of the letters that make up the encoded string. This is the process used by the aficionados of newspaper cryptograms. The cryptogram's solution is also greatly eased by maintaining the blanks between the words, which gives away a lot of information.

The encode-decode scheme here is quite different. Instead of substituting one letter for another, the subroutine scrambles the positions of the letters. The new letter positions are determined by displacing them a fixed number of positions, but the regularity of their shifts is not readily discernible. The original message is reproduced by reversing the shift procedure on the letters of the enciphered message.

REFERENCE:

One of us (JDR) created this position-shift algorithm after becoming intrigued with the encryption techniques described in an encyclopedia and searching for another application of prime numbers.

LISTING:

```
1000 ' **** cyclic prime code
1010 K8=K-P : L8=LEN(S$)
1020 IF L8-INT(L8/P)*P=0 THEN L8=L8+1
1030 S8$=STRING$(L8," ")
1040 FOR I8=1 TO L8
1050     K8=K8+P
1060     IF K8>L8 THEN K8=K8-L8
1070     IF N=1
           THEN MID$(S8$,I8,1)=MID$(S$,K8,1)
           ELSE MID$(S8$,K8,1)=MID$(S$,I8,1)
1080 NEXT I8
1090 S$=S8$
1100 RETURN
```

VARIABLES:

entering

```
S$:   Text to be encoded or decoded
P:    Prime number less than the length of S$
K:    Number less than the length of S$. Think of
      these numbers P and K as the passwords.
N:    Indicator for whether process is encoding
      (N=1) or decoding (N=0).
```

exiting

```
S$:   Encoded or decoded text
```

local

```
K8:   Interval for repositioning the character
L8:   Length of S$
I8:   Loop index
```

NOTES:

Line 1070 either transposes the K8th character to the I8th position if the indicator N asks for encoding, or transposes the I8th character to the K8th position if N asks for decoding. We could have written two subroutines instead of one, but we felt that this approach is more powerful and useful.

PROGRAM LISTING:

```
10 ' program : cyclic prime code : SS2CR1
20 ' authors : JOHN P GRILLO & JD ROBERTSON
30 '
40 CLEAR 1000
50 PRINT
60 PRINT "input text to be coded"
70 PRINT "  eg: don't hide carrots in the nasal cavity"
80 INPUT S$
90 IF S$="" THEN STOP
100 PRINT "input a prime number <";LEN(S$)
110 INPUT P
120 PRINT "input a number between 1 and";LEN(S$)
130 INPUT K
140 N=1
150 GOSUB 1000    ' <<<< call cyclic prime code
160 PRINT : PRINT S$
170 N=0
180 GOSUB 1000    ' <<<< call cyclic prime code
190 PRINT : PRINT S$
200 GOTO 50
1000 ' **** cyclic prime code
1010 K8=K-P : L8=LEN(S$)
1020 IF L8-INT(L8/P)*P=0 THEN L8=L8+1
1030 S8$=STRING$(L8," ")
1040 FOR I8=1 TO L8
1050    K8=K8+P
1060    IF K8>L8 THEN K8=K8-L8
1070    IF N=1
          THEN MID$(S8$,I8,1)=MID$(S$,K8,1)
          ELSE MID$(S8$,K8,1)=MID$(S$,I8,1)
1080 NEXT I8
1090 S$=S8$
1100 RETURN
9999 END
```

RUN:

```
input text to be coded
  eg: don't hide carrots in the nasal cavity
? never feed a duck with a machine gun
input a prime number < 36
? 23
input a number between 1 and 36
? 1

na gten rcue auheew hcvm n d ifikead

never feed a duck with a machine gun

input text to be coded
  eg: don't hide carrots in the nasal cavity
? never feed a duck with a machine gun
input a prime number < 36
? 23
input a number between 1 and 36
? 11

 gten rcue auheew hcvm n d ifikeadna

never feed a duck with a machine gun

input text to be coded
  eg: don't hide carrots in the nasal cavity
? never feed a duck with a machine gun
input a prime number < 36
? 17
input a number between 1 and 36
? 7

farhvin uc dnahdae   etewnkgue i cem

never feed a duck with a machine gun

input text to be coded
  eg: don't hide carrots in the nasal cavity
? never feed a duck with a machine gun
input a prime number < 36
? 31
input a number between 1 and 36
? 7

fe c   evghawdeeui iudrnnmtc  neahka

never feed a duck with a machine gun
```

Subroutine: Phrase Key Code SS2CR2

PURPOSE:

Encode or decode text by scrambling letter substitutions.

As was done in SS2CR1 previously, this subroutine uses the string of text passed to it as either plaintext to be encoded or code to be transformed into plaintext. This algorithm substitutes one of 37 characters for the original character in the message. The one chosen out of the 37 depends on both the password (the secret phrase supplied by the user) and the position of the characters. The effect is to produce an encoded string in which if the character "e" stands for the letter "w" at one place in the message, another "e" probably does not represent a "w" at another place in the message.

REFERENCE:

"Periodic polyalphabetic substitution," *Collier's Encyclopedia*, Vol. 7 (New York: Crowell Collier and Macmillan, 1967), pp. 523–525.

LISTING:

```
1000 ' **** phrase key code
1010 V$=" abcdefghijklmnopqrstuvwxyz0123456789"
1020 GOSUB 2000     ' <<<< call string clean-up & compress
1030 J8=0
1040 FOR I8=1 TO LEN(S$)
1050    J8=J8+1
1060    IF J8>LEN(P$) THEN J8=1
1070    S8=INSTR(V$,MID$(S$,I8,1))
1080    IF N=1
          THEN S8=S8+INSTR(V$,MID$(P$,J8,1))+10 :
               IF S8>37 THEN S8=S8-37 ELSE 1090
          ELSE S8=S8-INSTR(V$,MID$(P$,J8,1))-10 :
               IF S8<=0 THEN S8=S8+37
1090    MID$(S$,I8,1)=MID$(V$,S8,1)
1100 NEXT I8
1110 RETURN
```

VARIABLES:

```
entering

   S$:   Text to be encoded or decoded
   P$:   Password
   N:    Indicator for the process to be performed
         (if N=1, encode and if N=0, decode)

exiting

   S$:   Encoded or decoded text

local

   J8:   Counter
   I8:   Loop index
   S8:   Position of character substitution
   V$:   String of characters used for substitution
```

NOTES:

Line 1080 carries the burden of the work for this subroutine. It determines which character out of V$ is to be used, either to produce the code or to regenerate the original message. Line 1090 uses the MID$ to the left of the assignment symbol. See the Introduction to this volume for an alternative method of coding if your BASIC does not support this feature. This subroutine calls another, SS2WP1, which was described earlier in this volume in Chapter 4. The String Cleanup and Compress subroutine is used to make certain that all characters in the user's message can be encoded or decoded properly.

PROGRAM LISTING:

```
10 ' program : phrase key code : SS2CR2
20 ' authors : JOHN P GRILLO & JD ROBERTSON
30 '
40 CLEAR 1000
50 PRINT
60 PRINT "input text to be coded"
70 PRINT "  eg: rhubarb season will soon be upon us"
80 INPUT S$
90 IF S$="" THEN STOP
100 PRINT "input secret phrase"
110 INPUT P$
120 N=1
130 GOSUB 1000   ' <<<< call phrase key code
140 PRINT : PRINT S$
150 N=0
160 GOSUB 1000   ' <<<< call phrase key code
170 PRINT : PRINT S$
180 GOTO 50
1000 ' **** phrase key code
1010 V$=" abcdefghijklmnopqrstuvwxyz0123456789"
1020 GOSUB 2000   ' <<<< call string clean-up & compress
1030 J8=0
1040 FOR I8=1 TO LEN(S$)
1050    J8=J8+1
1060    IF J8>LEN(P$) THEN J8=1
1070    S8=INSTR(V$,MID$(S$,I8,1))
1080    IF N=1
          THEN S8=S8+INSTR(V$,MID$(P$,J8,1))+10 :
               IF S8>37 THEN S8=S8-37 ELSE 1090
          ELSE S8=S8-INSTR(V$,MID$(P$,J8,1))-10 :
               IF S8<=0 THEN S8=S8+37
1090    MID$(S$,I8,1)=MID$(V$,S8,1)
1100 NEXT I8
1110 RETURN
2000 ' #### string clean-up & compress
2010 S8$=""
2020 FOR I8=1 TO LEN(S$)
2030    IF INSTR(V$,MID$(S$,I8,1))<>0
          THEN S8$=S8$+MID$(S$,I8,1)
2040 NEXT I8
2050 S$=S8$
2060 RETURN
9999 END
```

RUN:

```
input text to be coded
  eg: rhubarb season will soon be upon us
? the echidna is a monotreme
input secret phrase
? chelmsford

70uw26y862osyex4qbg22b71 8

the echidna is a monotreme

input text to be coded
  eg: rhubarb season will soon be upon us
? the echidna is a monotreme
input secret phrase
? waltham

qt14xo5fp 5suf7mwg7zbq31gx

the echidna is a monotreme

input text to be coded
  eg: rhubarb season will soon be upon us
? the platypus is also a monotreme
input secret phrase
? massachusetts

gt831ztor5om36434x6754pgigb5k8ys

the platypus is also a monotreme

input text to be coded
  eg: rhubarb season will soon be upon us
? the platypus is also a monotreme
input secret phrase
? new hampshire

hxbk8xyjr8dkp787144b04s6g3c9op5q

the platypus is also a monotreme

input text to be coded
  eg: rhubarb season will soon be upon us
? marsupials are more fun than people
input secret phrase
? what

jt3mr8u5ial5oxlgl q4ccz4q0mh78qim4q

marsupials are more fun than people
```

Subroutine: Rail-Fence Code SS2CR3

PURPOSE:

Encode or decode text by shifting letters.

The rail-fence code was used during the Civil War. Its charm is the eerie almost-readable output code. As in the cyclic prime code shown in SS2CR1 earlier, the encoded message is made up of the original letters in mixed order. However, the rail-fence code's letter shifts are always halfway down the message, which tends to keep the word sizes the same.

REFERENCE:

"Rail-fence code," *Collier's Encyclopedia*, Vol. 7 (New York: Crowell Collier and Macmillan, 1967), p. 519.

LISTING:

```
1000 ' **** rail-fence code
1010 L8=LEN(S$)
1020 IF L8<>INT(L8/2)*2
       THEN S$=S$+" " : L8=L8+1
1030 S8$=STRING$(L8," ")
1040 M8=L8/2 : J8=0
1050 FOR I8=1 TO L8 STEP 2
1060     J8=J8+1
1070     IF N=1
           THEN MID$(S8$,I8,1)=MID$(S$,J8,1) :
                MID$(S8$,I8+1,1)=MID$(S$,J8+M8,1)
           ELSE MID$(S8$,J8,1)=MID$(S$,I8,1) :
                MID$(S8$,J8+M8,1)=MID$(S$,I8+1,1)
1080 NEXT I8
1090 S$=S8$
1100 RETURN
```

VARIABLES:

```
entering

   S$:   Text to be encoded or decoded
   N:    Indicator for encoding or decoding (N=1 or 0)

exiting

   S$:   Encoded or decoded text

local

   L8:   Length of S$
   S8$:  Temporary storage for exiting string
   M8:   Displacement for even characters
   I8:   Loop index
   J8:   Position of substitution
```

NOTES:

No passwords! The user inputs text and the algorithm uses the length of the string as its position finder for substitutions.

Line 1020 forces the entered string to have an even length. This is necessary to be sure to encode (or decode) the last character.

This method of scrambling a message is hardly secure. You can decode any message visually by reading every other letter. When you get to the end of the message, simply continue reading it starting at the second letter.

PROGRAM LISTING:

```
10 ' program : rail-fence code : SS2CR3
20 ' authors : JOHN P GRILLO & JD ROBERTSON
30 '
40 CLEAR 1000
50 PRINT
60 PRINT "input text to be coded"
70 PRINT "  eg: burpless cucumbers often are not"
80 INPUT S$
90 IF S$="" THEN STOP
100 N=1
110 GOSUB 1000   ' <<<< call rail-fence code
120 PRINT : PRINT S$
130 N=0
140 GOSUB 1000   ' <<<< call rail-fence code
150 PRINT : PRINT S$
160 GOTO 50
1000 ' **** rail-fence code
1010 L8=LEN(S$)
1020 IF L8<>INT(L8/2)*2
       THEN S$=S$+" " : L8=L8+1
1030 S8$=STRING$(L8," ")
1040 M8=L8/2 : J8=0
1050 FOR I8=1 TO L8 STEP 2
1060    J8=J8+1
1070    IF N=1
          THEN MID$(S8$,I8,1)=MID$(S$,J8,1) :
               MID$(S8$,I8+1,1)=MID$(S$,J8+M8,1)
          ELSE MID$(S8$,J8,1)=MID$(S$,I8,1) :
               MID$(S8$,J8+M8,1)=MID$(S$,I8+1,1)
1080 NEXT I8
1090 S$=S8$
1100 RETURN
9999 END
```

RUN:

```
input text to be coded
  eg: burpless cucumbers often are not
? multiflora means many-flowered

msu lmtainfyl-ofrlao wmeeraend

multiflora means many-flowered
```

RUN (CONTINUED):

```
input text to be coded
  eg: burpless cucumbers often are not
? columbine are graceful and airy plants

cfoullu mabnidn ea iarrye  pglraanctes

columbine are graceful and airy plants

input text to be coded
  eg: burpless cucumbers often are not
? calliopsis are bright and daisy-like

cgahltl iaonpds idsa iasrye- lbirkie

calliopsis are bright and daisy-like

input text to be coded
  eg: burpless cucumbers often are not
? nicotiana are excellent bedding plants

nliecnott ibaendad ianrge  pelxacnetls

nicotiana are excellent bedding plants

input text to be coded
  eg: burpless cucumbers often are not
? caladium are a popular foliage plant

cuallaard ifuoml iaargee  ap lpaonpt

caladium are a popular foliage plant

input text to be coded
  eg: burpless cucumbers often are not
? vinca (periwinkle) have large single blossoms

v ilnacrag e( pseirnigwlien kblleo)s shoamvse

vinca (periwinkle) have large single blossoms

input text to be coded
  eg: burpless cucumbers often are not
? chrysanthemums are a traditional autumn favorite

cdhirtyisoannatlh eamuutmusm na rfea vao rtirtae

chrysanthemums are a traditional autumn favorite

input text to be coded
  eg: burpless cucumbers often are not
? what can be said about salpiglossis

wbhoautt  csaanl pbieg lsoasisdi sa

what can be said about salpiglossis
```

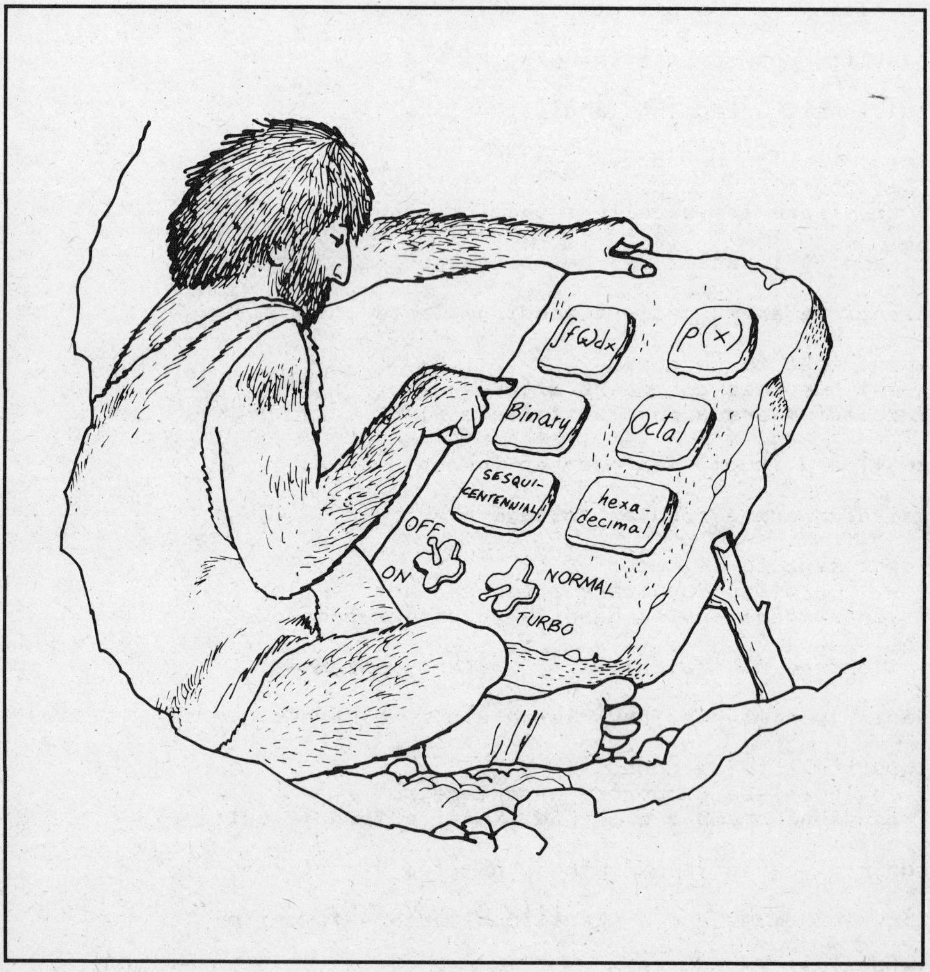

∫f(x)dx
p(x)
Binary
Octal
SESQUI-
CENTENNIAL
hexa-
decimal
OFF
ON
NORMAL
TURBO

CHAPTER

6

$\int \frac{dy}{dx}$

MATHEMATICS

Introduction

The seven subroutines that you will find in this section represent three different areas in the discipline of mathematics. The first three subroutines, MA1, MA2, and MA3, all deal with the problem of converting a number from some base other than 10 to base 10. They are useful in understanding computer arithmetic, certainly, but they have other more subtle applications. You could encode salary information in, say, base 27; you could compress data (a 10-digit base-10 value would take up 6 or 7 digits in base 30); you could invent mnemonics for large numbers: What is DDT-base-36 in base 10?

The second set of three subroutines show some classic techniques used by students in numerical methods courses to evaluate polynomials and to integrate transcendental functions. As with any other subroutine, you need an application to use these.

The last subroutine, MA7, is a statistical data reduction method that transforms a number of points scattered over a grid into a line. A common application of this technique is in trend analysis, where you have existing data points from which you want to derive future performance.

Subroutine: Binary-to-Decimal Conversion SS2MA1

PURPOSE:

Convert a binary number to base 10.

In the first volume of Subroutine Sandwich, we supplied you with the complement of this routine. That one converted a decimal number to base 2. Here we do the reverse.

The user supplies a binary number, which the program assumes to be a string made up of ones and zeros. All entered numbers are assumed to be positive integers.

REFERENCE:

J. W. Estes and B. R. Ellis, *Elements of Computer Science* (New York: Harper & Row, 1973), p. 90.

LISTING:

```
1000 ' **** binary to decimal conversion
1010 D=0
1020 FOR I8=1 TO LEN(N$)
1030    D=INSTR("01",MID$(N$,I8,1))-1+D+D
1040 NEXT I8
1050 RETURN
```

VARIABLES:

```
entering

   N$:    Binary integer as a string of 1s and 0s

exiting

   D:     Decimal integer

local

   I8:    Loop index
```

NOTES:

This subroutine uses the INSTR function to isolate both the value and the position of each bit. Line 1030 looks at the first bit: If it is "0", D is 0; if it is "1", D is 1. Then each successive bit is scanned from left to right. As long as there is another bit, the amount D is doubled and a 1 or a 0 is added to it depending on the value of that bit.

11101011010010001.... ⟶ 2742039554....

PROGRAM LISTING:

```
10 ' program : binary to decimal conversion : SS2MA1
20 ' authors : JOHN P GRILLO & JD ROBERTSON
30 '
40 PRINT
50 PRINT "input binary integer"
60 INPUT N$
70 IF N$="" THEN STOP
80 GOSUB 1000    ' <<<< call binary to decimal conversion
90 PRINT N$;" (2) = ";D;"(10)"
100 GOTO 40
1000 ' **** binary to decimal conversion
1010 D=0
1020 FOR I8=1 TO LEN(N$)
1030    D=INSTR("01",MID$(N$,I8,1))-1+D+D
1040 NEXT I8
1050 RETURN
9999 END
```

RUN:

```
input binary integer
? 1001101
1001101 (2) =  77 (10)

input binary integer
? 1001000111110
1001000111110 (2) =  4670 (10)

input binary integer
? 1111111111111111
1111111111111111 (2) =  65535 (10)

input binary integer
? 101010
101010 (2) =  42 (10)

input binary integer
? 1010100
1010100 (2) =  84 (10)

input binary integer
? 10101000
10101000 (2) =  168 (10)

input binary integer
? 1
1 (2) =  1 (10)

input binary integer
? 10
10 (2) =  2 (10)
```

RUN (CONTINUED):

```
input binary integer
? 11
11 (2) =  3 (10)

input binary integer
? 100
100 (2) =  4 (10)

input binary integer
? 101
101 (2) =  5 (10)

input binary integer
? 110
110 (2) =  6 (10)

input binary integer
? 111
111 (2) =  7 (10)

input binary integer
? 1000
1000 (2) =  8 (10)

input binary integer
? 1001
1001 (2) =  9 (10)

input binary integer
? 1010
1010 (2) =  10 (10)

input binary integer
? 1011
1011 (2) =  11 (10)

input binary integer
? 1100
1100 (2) =  12 (10)

input binary integer
? 1101
1101 (2) =  13 (10)

input binary integer
? 1110
1110 (2) =  14 (10)

input binary integer
? 1111
1111 (2) =  15 (10)
```

Subroutine: Hexadecimal-to-Decimal Conversion SS2MA2

PURPOSE:

Convert a hexadecimal integer to base 10.

In this subroutine, the entering value (again represented as a string, as in SS2MA1 previously) is a hexadecimal, or base-16 number. The output is its decimal equivalent. Thus if "A" is entered, 10 is produced, and if the string "FF" is entered, the value 255 is returned.

REFERENCE:

Encyclopedia of Computer Science, Anthony Ralston, Ed. (New York: Van Nostrand Reinhold, 1976), p. 969.

SUBROUTINE LISTING:

```
1000 ' **** hexadecimal to decimal conversion
1010 H8$="0123456789ABCDEF"
1020 D=0
1030 FOR I8=1 TO LEN(N$)
1040     D=INSTR(H8$,MID$(N$,I8,1))-1+16*D
1050 NEXT I8
1060 RETURN
```

VARIABLES:

```
entering

   N$:    Hexadecimal integer

exiting

   D:     Decimal value equivalent to N$

local

   H8$:   Hexadecimal digits 0 to F
   I8:    Loop index
```

NOTES:

Neither this subroutine nor the preceding one, SS2MA1, the binary-to-decimal converter, does any validation of this input. The assumption in both cases is that the user has entered legal binary or hexadecimal values as strings.

Notice the strong resemblance between this code and the code in the previous subroutine. We consider this high degree of likeness to indicate one of the strong points of good subroutines. The schemes are so general in nature that they can be adapted (to new number bases in this case) with relative ease.

3AB290CFB.... ⟶ 3498226504...

PROGRAM LISTING:

```
10 ' program : hexadecimal to decimal conversion : SS2MA2
20 ' authors : JOHN P GRILLO & JD ROBERTSON
30 '
40 PRINT
50 PRINT "input hexadecimal integer"
60 INPUT N$
70 IF N$="" THEN STOP
80 GOSUB 1000    ' <<<< call hexadecimal to decimal conversion
90 PRINT N$;" (16) = ";D;"(10)"
100 GOTO 40
1000 ' **** hexadecimal to decimal conversion
1010 H8$="0123456789ABCDEF"
1020 D=0
1030 FOR I8=1 TO LEN(N$)
1040     D=INSTR(H8$,MID$(N$,I8,1))-1+16*D
1050 NEXT I8
1060 RETURN
9999 END
```

RUN:

```
input hexadecimal integer
? 4D
4D (16) =  77 (10)

input hexadecimal integer
? 123E
123E (16) =  4670 (10)

input hexadecimal integer
? FFFF
FFFF (16) =  65535 (10)

input hexadecimal integer
? 2A
2A (16) =  42 (10)

input hexadecimal integer
? 54
54 (16) =  84 (10)

input hexadecimal integer
? A8
A8 (16) =  168 (10)

input hexadecimal integer
? 1
1 (16) =  1 (10)

input hexadecimal integer
? 2
2 (16) =  2 (10)
```

RUN (CONTINUED):

```
input hexadecimal integer
? 3
3 (16) =  3 (10)

input hexadecimal integer
? 4
4 (16) =  4 (10)

input hexadecimal integer
? 5
5 (16) =  5 (10)

input hexadecimal integer
? 6
6 (16) =  6 (10)

input hexadecimal integer
? 7
7 (16) =  7 (10)

input hexadecimal integer
? 8
8 (16) =  8 (10)

input hexadecimal integer
? 9
9 (16) =  9 (10)

input hexadecimal integer
? A
A (16) =  10 (10)

input hexadecimal integer
? B
B (16) =  11 (10)

input hexadecimal integer
? C
C (16) =  12 (10)

input hexadecimal integer
? D
D (16) =  13 (10)

input hexadecimal integer
? E
E (16) =  14 (10)

input hexadecimal integer
? F
F (16) =  15 (10)

input hexadecimal integer
? 10
10 (16) =  16 (10)
```

Subroutine: Base-N-to-Decimal-Conversion SS2MA3

PURPOSE:

Convert a number in any base to base 10.

Actually, there is a limit of 36 to the entering number base. The way this routine is written, the user makes two entries: The first entry is a value that represents the base of the number to be converted to decimal; the second entry is a string of digits that represent the base-N number to be converted to decimal.

REFERENCE:

Donald Knuth, "Seminumerical Algorithms," *The Art of Computer Programming*, Vol. 2 (Reading, MA: Addison-Wesley, 1969).

SUBROUTINE LISTING:

```
1000 ' **** base-n to decimal conversion
1010 H8$="0123456789ABCDEFGHIJKLMNOPQRSTUVWXYZ"
1020 D=0
1030 FOR I8=1 TO LEN(N$)
1040     D=INSTR(H8$,MID$(N$,I8,1))-1+B*D
1050 NEXT I8
1060 RETURN
```

VARIABLES:

entering

B: Base of number to be converted
N$: Number to be converted, entered as a string

exiting

D: Value of N$ in base 10

local

H8$: Characters to represent the digits in base N
I8: Loop index

NOTES:

This clone to the previous two subroutines further exemplifies the degree to which some of these subroutines can be generalized. The most important difference between this and the other two subroutines is in line 1040. At the end of that line you see that every time a new digit is found the previous sum is increased by B*D. This corresponds to the notion of place notation for all numbers. If you read the number from right to left, every digit represents a value of that digit multiplied by the base taken to a power determined by the position.

RJ9KLUVON5.... ⟶ 308972558432...

PROGRAM LISTING:

```
10 ' program : base-n to decimal conversion : SS2MA3
20 ' authors : JOHN P GRILLO & JD ROBERTSON
30 '
40 PRINT
50 PRINT "input base"
60 INPUT B
70 IF B=0 THEN STOP
80 PRINT "input base";B;"integer"
90 INPUT N$
100 GOSUB 1000    ' <<<< call base-n to decimal conversion
110 PRINT N$;" (";RIGHT$(STR$(B),LEN(STR$(B))-1);")=";D;"(10)"
120 GOTO 40
1000 ' **** base-n to decimal conversion
1010 H8$="0123456789ABCDEFGHIJKLMNOPQRSTUVWXYZ"
1020 D=0
1030 FOR I8=1 TO LEN(N$)
1040     D=INSTR(H8$,MID$(N$,I8,1))-1+B*D
1050 NEXT I8
1060 RETURN
9999 END
```

RUN:

```
input base
? 2
input base 2 integer
? 110001110101
110001110101 (2)= 3189 (10)

input base
? 8
input base 8 integer
? 6165
6165 (8)= 3189 (10)

input base
? 16
input base 16 integer
? C75
C75 (16)= 3189 (10)

input base
? 30
input base 30 integer
? 3G9
3G9 (30)= 3189 (10)

input base
? 17
input base 17 integer
? ABE
ABE (17)= 3091 (10)
```

RUN (CONTINUED):

```
input base
? 36
input base 36 integer
? JOHN
JOHN (36)= 918203 (10)

input base
? 36
input base 36 integer
? BETSY
BETSY (36)= 1.91676E+07 (10)

input base
? 36
input base 36 integer
? CELIA
CELIA (36)= 2.08365E+07 (10)

input base
? 36
input base 36 integer
? DOUG
DOUG (36)= 638728 (10)

input base
? 4
input base 4 integer
? 10
10 (4)= 4 (10)

input base
? 8
input base 8 integer
? 10
10 (8)= 8 (10)

input base
? 12
input base 12 integer
? 10
10 (12)= 12 (10)

input base
? 27
input base 27 integer
? 10
10 (27)= 27 (10)

input base
? 16
input base 16 integer
? ABE
ABE (16)= 2750 (10)
```

Subroutine: Horner's Method SS2MA4

PURPOSE:

Evaluate an order-N polynomial.

Horner's method of evaluating a polynomial is straightforward. Given the degree of the polynomial (the highest power of X contained in the polynomial) and given the coefficients for each term in the polynomial, the process is one of substitution and term-by-term calculation. The calling program supplies the degree and the term's coefficients, the argument for the polynomial (the value of X for which the polynomial is to be evaluated), and the subroutine returns the value of the polynomial.

REFERENCE:

Peter Stark, *Introduction to Numerical Methods* (New York: Macmillan, 1970), pp. 103–110.

LISTING:

```
1000 ' **** Horner's method
1010 P=A(N+1)
1020 IF N=0 THEN RETURN
1030 FOR I8=N TO 1 STEP -1
1040    P=A(I8)+X*P
1050 NEXT I8
1060 RETURN
```

VARIABLES:

```
entering

    A:  List of coefficients, in order from constant
        through higher degrees
    N:  Degree of the polynomial
    X:  Argument of the polynomial


exiting

    P:  Value of the polynomial for argument X


local

    I8:  Loop index
```

NOTES:

The calling program must be sure to supply the coefficients for all of the terms, including the zeros for the terms not included in the polynomial. For example, the coefficients for the polynomial $5 + 2x - 3x^3$ are 5, 2, 0, and –3.

The subroutine works from the highest term to the lowest. In the example above, the first calculation (with X=4, for example) produces 0+4*(–3)=–12. The next iteration produces 2+4*(–12)=– 46. The last, 5+4*(– 46)=–179.

PROGRAM LISTING:

```
10 ' program : Horner's method : SS2MA4
20 ' authors : JOHN P GRILLO & JD ROBERTSON
30 '
40 DIM A(10)
50 INPUT "input degree of polynomial < 10";N
60 FOR I=1 TO N+1
70    PRINT "input coefficient of x ↑";I-1
80    INPUT A(I)
90 NEXT I
100 PRINT
110 PRINT "p( X ) = ";A(1);
120 FOR I=1 TO N
130   IF A(I+1)<0
        THEN PRINT " -";
        ELSE PRINT " +";
140     PRINT " X *(";ABS(A(I+1));
150 NEXT I
160 PRINT STRING$(N,")")
170 INPUT "polynomial is to be evaluated with what argument X";X
180 GOSUB 1000    ' <<<< call Horner's method
190 PRINT "p(";X;") = ";P;
200 PRINT
210 PRINT "continue ..."
220 FOR I=1 TO 200
230     IF INKEY$<>"" THEN 100
240 NEXT I
250 STOP
1000 ' **** Horner's method
1010 P=A(N+1)
1020 IF N=0 THEN RETURN
1030 FOR I8=N TO 1 STEP -1
1040     P=A(I8)+X*P
1050 NEXT I8
1060 RETURN
9999 END
```

RUN:

```
input degree of polynomial < 10? 3
input coefficient of x ↑ 0
? -1
input coefficient of x ↑ 1
? 2
input coefficient of x ↑ 2
? 0
input coefficient of x ↑ 3
? 1

p( X ) = -1  + X *( 2  + X *( 0  + X *( 1 )))
polynomial is to be evaluated with what argument X? -1
p(-1 ) = -4
continue ...

p( X ) = -1  + X *( 2  + X *( 0  + X *( 1 )))
polynomial is to be evaluated with what argument X? 0
p( 0 ) = -1
continue ...

p( X ) = -1  + X *( 2  + X *( 0  + X *( 1 )))
polynomial is to be evaluated with what argument X? 1
p( 1 ) =  2
continue ...

p( X ) = -1  + X *( 2  + X *( 0  + X *( 1 )))
polynomial is to be evaluated with what argument X? 1.3
p( 1.3 ) =  3.797
continue ...

p( X ) = -1  + X *( 2  + X *( 0  + X *( 1 )))
polynomial is to be evaluated with what argument X? 1.8
p( 1.8 ) =  8.432
continue ...

p( X ) = -1  + X *( 2  + X *( 0  + X *( 1 )))
polynomial is to be evaluated with what argument X? 5
p( 5 ) =  134
continue ...

p( X ) = -1  + X *( 2  + X *( 0  + X *( 1 )))
polynomial is to be evaluated with what argument X? 10
p( 10 ) =  1019
continue ...

p( X ) = -1  + X *( 2  + X *( 0  + X *( 1 )))
polynomial is to be evaluated with what argument X? 10.1
p( 10.1 ) =  1049.5
continue ...
```

Subroutine: Trapezoidal Rule SS2MA5

PURPOSE:

Approximate the integral of a function.

The trapezoidal rule is one of the several common procedures used to calculate the integral of a function. It is based on a successively closer approximation of the true area under a curve by subdividing that area into a series of trapezoids.

This subroutine calculates the integral after the calling program provides the number of intervals on which to base the approximation. The calling program supplies the function as FNC, the two integration limits, and the number of subintervals. The single value returned represents the area of all subinterval trapezoids.

REFERENCE:

Louis Kelly, *Handbook of Numerical Methods and Applications* (Reading, MA.: Addison-Wesley, 1967), pp. 54–55.

SUBROUTINE LISTING:

```
1000 ' **** trapezoidal rule
1010 H8=(B-A)/N
1020 T=FNC(A)+FNC(B)
1030 IF N=1 THEN 1070
1040 FOR I8=2 TO N
1050    T=T+2*FNC(A+(I8-1)*H8)
1060 NEXT I8
1070 T=T*H8/2
1080 RETURN
```

VARIABLES:

```
entering

    A,B:   Lower and upper integration limits
    N:     Number of subintervals
    FNC:   User-defined function to be integrated

exiting

    T:     Approximation of the integral using
           the trapezoidal rule

local

    H8:    Base of trapezoid, calculated as integration
           width divided by N
    I8:    Loop index
```

NOTES:

In order to understand the way this subroutine works, you should trace it through a simple iteration using a simple function, as in this program, and a small set of subintervals. You will see how increasing the number of subintervals more closely approximates the true area under the curve.

An important difference between this subroutine and most others is that one of the entering items is a function defined in the calling program. BASIC is especially useful in this regard because all variables and user-defined functions are global rather than local. Global variables are the same both in the main program and in the subroutines. Local variables exist only within a given program or subroutine.

PROGRAM LISTING:

```
10 ' program : trapezoidal rule : SS2MA5
20 ' authors : JOHN P GRILLO & JD ROBERTSON
30 '
40 DEF FNC(X)=X↑4
50 PRINT
60 INPUT "input integration limits";A,B
70 INPUT "input number of subintervals";N
80 GOSUB 1000    ' <<<< call trapezoidal rule
90 PRINT
100 PRINT "trapezoidal rule approx to integral of function"
110 PRINT "from";A;"to";B;"using";N;"subintervals is";T
120 FOR I=1 TO 200
130    IF INKEY$<>"" THEN 50
140 NEXT I
150 STOP
1000 ' **** trapezoidal rule
1010 H8=(B-A)/N
1020 T=FNC(A)+FNC(B)
1030 IF N=1 THEN 1070
1040 FOR I8=2 TO N
1050    T=T+2*FNC(A+(I8-1)*H8)
1060 NEXT I8
1070 T=T*H8/2
1080 RETURN
9999 END
```

RUN:

```
input integration limits? 2,5
input number of subintervals? 2

trapezoidal rule approx to integral of function
from 2 to 5 using 2 subintervals is 705.844

input integration limits? 2,5
input number of subintervals? 20

trapezoidal rule approx to integral of function
from 2 to 5 using 20 subintervals is 619.478
```

RUN (CONTINUED):

```
input integration limits? 0,4
input number of subintervals? 1

trapezoidal rule approx to integral of function
from 0 to 4 using 1 subintervals is 512

input integration limits? 0,4
input number of subintervals? 2

trapezoidal rule approx to integral of function
from 0 to 4 using 2 subintervals is 288

input integration limits? 0,4
input number of subintervals? 10

trapezoidal rule approx to integral of function
from 0 to 4 using 10 subintervals is 208.21

input integration limits? 0,4
input number of subintervals? 20

trapezoidal rule approx to integral of function
from 0 to 4 using 20 subintervals is 205.653

input integration limits? 0,4
input number of subintervals? 50

trapezoidal rule approx to integral of function
from 0 to 4 using 50 subintervals is 204.937

input integration limits? 0,4
input number of subintervals? 100

trapezoidal rule approx to integral of function
from 0 to 4 using 100 subintervals is 204.834

input integration limits? 0,4
input number of subintervals? 199

trapezoidal rule approx to integral of function
from 0 to 4 using 199 subintervals is 204.809
```

Subroutine: Simpson's Rule SS2MA6

PURPOSE:

Calculate the integral of a function.

This subroutine is similar to the previous one, the trapezoidal rule calculation of an integral. However, this one approximates the area using a series of rectangularly shaped panels rather than a series of trapezoids. The accuracy of this approach depends upon the number of panels.

The calling program supplies the function in the form of a user-defined function. The limits of integration and the number of panels is also entered by the user and passed to the subroutine.

REFERENCE:

Louis Kelly, *Handbook of Numerical Methods and Applications* (Reading, MA.: Addison-Wesley, 1967), pp. 54–55.

LISTING:

```
1000 ' **** Simpson's rule
1010 H8=(B-A)/(N*2)
1020 S=FNC(A)+FNC(B)+4*FNC(B-H8)
1030 IF N=1 THEN 1070
1040 FOR I8=2 TO 2*N-1 STEP 2
1050    S=S+4*FNC(A+(I8-1)*H8)+2*FNC(A+I8*H8
1060 NEXT I8
1070 S=S*H8/3
1080 RETURN
```

VARIABLES:

```
entering

   A,B:   Limits of integration
   N:     Number of panels
   FNC:   User-defined function that corresponds to
          the function to be integrated

exiting

   S:     Approximation of the integral using
          Simpson's rule

local

   H8:    Area of a panel
   I8:    Loop index
```

NOTES:

Simpson's rule produces a more accurate approximation than the trapezoidal rule because its derivation uses a second-degree polynomial rather than the first-degree function used in the derivation of the trapezoidal rule. We recommend that you consult a numerical analysis text, such as the one cited above, if you wish to study this technique further.

PROGRAM LISTING:

```
10 ' program : Simpson's rule : SS2MA6
20 ' authors : JOHN P GRILLO & JD ROBERTSON
30 '
40 DEF FNC(X)=X↑4
50 PRINT
60 INPUT "input integration limits";A,B
70 INPUT "input number of panels";N
80 GOSUB 1000    ' <<<< call Simpson's rule
90 PRINT
100 PRINT "Simpson's rule approx to integral of function"
110 PRINT "from";A;"to";B;"using";N;"panels is";S
120 FOR I=1 TO 200
130     IF INKEY$<>"" THEN 50
140 NEXT I
150 STOP
1000 ' **** Simpson's rule
1010 H8=(B-A)/(N*2)
1020 S=FNC(A)+FNC(B)+4*FNC(B-H8)
1030 IF N=1 THEN 1070
1040 FOR I8=2 TO 2*N-1 STEP 2
1050     S=S+4*FNC(A+(I8-1)*H8)+2*FNC(A+I8*H8)
1060 NEXT I8
1070 S=S*H8/3
1080 RETURN
9999 END
```

RUN:

```
input integration limits? 2,5
input number of panels? 2

Simpson's rule approx to integral of function
from 2 to 5 using 2 panels is 618.727

input integration limits? 2,5
input number of panels? 10

Simpson's rule approx to integral of function
from 2 to 5 using 10 panels is 618.601
```

RUN (CONTINUED):

```
input integration limits? 0,4
input number of panels? 1

Simpson's rule approx to integral of function
from 0 to 4 using 1 panels is 213.333

input integration limits? 0,4
input number of panels? 2

Simpson's rule approx to integral of function
from 0 to 4 using 2 panels is 205.333

input integration limits? 0,4
input number of panels? 5

Simpson's rule approx to integral of function
from 0 to 4 using 5 panels is 204.814

input integration limits? 0,4
input number of panels? 10

Simpson's rule approx to integral of function
from 0 to 4 using 10 panels is 204.801

input integration limits? 0,4
input number of panels? 20

Simpson's rule approx to integral of function
from 0 to 4 using 20 panels is 204.8

input integration limits? 0,4
input number of panels? 50

Simpson's rule approx to integral of function
from 0 to 4 using 50 panels is 204.8

input integration limits? 0,4
input number of panels? 100

Simpson's rule approx to integral of function
from 0 to 4 using 100 panels is 204.8
```

Subroutine: Linear Least-Squares Fit SS2MA7

PURPOSE:

Calculate the equation of the straight line that best fits a set of numeric data.

One of the common statistical techniques used in financial or market trend analysis is to produce the straight line that best fits a set of data. The method is based on minimizing the sum-of-squares errors between the line and the x-y coordinates of the data points.

Most trend analysis procedures use the linear least-squares fit straight line as a predictor for future activities, such as profits, sales, or academic success.

REFERENCE:

Byron Gottfried, *Programming with BASIC*, Schaum's Outline Series (New York: McGraw-Hill, 1975), p. 194.

SUBROUTINE LISTING:

```
1000 ' **** linear least squares fit
1010 S8=0 : S9=0
1020 T8=0 : T9=0
1030 FOR I8=1 TO N
1040     S8=S8+X(I8) : S9=S9+X(I8)↑2
1050     T8=T8+Y(I8) : T9=T9+X(I8)*Y(I8)
1060 NEXT I8
1070 M=(N*T9-S8*T8)/(N*S9-S8↑2)
1080 B=(S9*T8-S8*T9)/(N*S9-S8↑2)
1090 RETURN
```

VARIABLES:

```
entering

    X:  Table of x values
    Y:  Table of y values
    N:  Number of x and y points

exiting

    M:  Slope of least-squares fit line
    B:  y-intercept of least-squares fit line

local

    S8:  Sum of x errors
    S9:  Sum of x-squared errors
    T8:  Sum of y errors
    T9:  Sum of x-y (cross-product) errors
    I8:  Loop index
```

NOTES:

Pearson's product-moment correlation coefficient calculation is a closely related procedure. In fact, you could calculate the correlation coefficient in one statement after having done all the work in lines 1010 through 1060. We have elected to keep the two algorithms separate because the two are not commonly used together, and their applications are quite different.

PROGRAM LISTING:

```
10 ' program : linear least squares fit : SS2MA7
20 ' authors : JOHN P GRILLO & JD ROBERTSON
30 '
40 DIM X(60),Y(60)
50 N=10+RND(50)
60 PRINT N;"data points (x,y)" : PRINT
70 FOR I=1 TO N
80    X(I)=I : Y(I)=X(I)-5+RND(9)
90    PRINT "(";X(I);",";Y(I);")",
100 NEXT I
110 GOSUB 1000   ' <<<< call linear least squares fit
120 PRINT : PRINT
130 PRINT "least squares line" : PRINT
140 PRINT "y = ";M;"x";
150 IF B<0
      THEN PRINT " -";
      ELSE PRINT " +";
160 PRINT ABS(B)
170 STOP
1000 ' **** linear least squares fit
1010 S8=0 : S9=0
1020 T8=0 : T9=0
1030 FOR I8=1 TO N
1040    S8=S8+X(I8) : S9=S9+X(I8)↑2
1050    T8=T8+Y(I8) : T9=T9+X(I8)*Y(I8)
1060 NEXT I8
1070 M=(N*T9-S8*T8)/(N*S9-S8↑2)
1080 B=(S9*T8-S8*T9)/(N*S9-S8↑2)
1090 RETURN
9999 END
```

RUN:

```
 11 data points (x,y)

( 1 ,-1 )        ( 2 , 0 )        ( 3 , 4 )        ( 4 , 4 )
( 5 , 1 )        ( 6 , 5 )        ( 7 , 8 )        ( 8 , 10 )
( 9 , 7 )        ( 10 , 11 )      ( 11 , 8 )

least squares line

y =  1.06363 x - 1.19999
```

RUN (CONTINUED):

```
 38 data points (x,y)

( 1 , 3 )         ( 2 , 1 )         ( 3 ,-1 )         ( 4 , 1 )
( 5 , 9 )         ( 6 , 9 )         ( 7 , 11 )        ( 8 , 9 )
( 9 , 7 )         ( 10 , 12 )       ( 11 , 10 )       ( 12 , 8 )
( 13 , 17 )       ( 14 , 17 )       ( 15 , 19 )       ( 16 , 16 )
( 17 , 19 )       ( 18 , 16 )       ( 19 , 20 )       ( 20 , 19 )
( 21 , 17 )       ( 22 , 26 )       ( 23 , 26 )       ( 24 , 28 )
( 25 , 23 )       ( 26 , 27 )       ( 27 , 26 )       ( 28 , 26 )
( 29 , 31 )       ( 30 , 34 )       ( 31 , 31 )       ( 32 , 28 )
( 33 , 30 )       ( 34 , 31 )       ( 35 , 34 )       ( 36 , 33 )
( 37 , 34 )       ( 38 , 38 )

least squares line

y =  .939381 x + 1.28736


 14 data points (x,y)

( 1 , 2 )         ( 2 , 5 )         ( 3 , 1 )         ( 4 , 1 )
( 5 , 5 )         ( 6 , 4 )         ( 7 , 8 )         ( 8 , 7 )
( 9 , 9 )         ( 10 , 7 )        ( 11 , 15 )       ( 12 , 15 )
( 13 , 16 )       ( 14 , 16 )

least squares line

y =  1.21099 x - 1.15384


 19 data points (x,y)

( 1 , 4 )         ( 2 , 0 )         ( 3 , 5 )         ( 4 , 8 )
( 5 , 7 )         ( 6 , 4 )         ( 7 , 9 )         ( 8 , 4 )
( 9 , 9 )         ( 10 , 12 )       ( 11 , 9 )        ( 12 , 9 )
( 13 , 16 )       ( 14 , 15 )       ( 15 , 17 )       ( 16 , 14 )
( 17 , 13 )       ( 18 , 16 )       ( 19 , 18 )

least squares line

y =  .826315 x + 1.68422
```

CHAPTER

7

TABLE MANAGEMENT

Introduction

Several processes are fundamental to the area of information processing. One of these is sorting, which is simply the arrangement of data into either ascending or descending order. Many computers have spent many hours in performing this seemingly simple task. As you will see when you experiment with the several algorithms for sorting that we have given you here, some are better than others.

There is little likelihood that the users of computer output will stop writing or reading sorted lists. Those lists are produced for better readability or for faster access. The sorting of data is a process that will remain useful, so we caution you to use a reasonable sort for the application.

Subroutine: Delayed Replacement Sort SS2TM1

PURPOSE:

Arrange a list of values into ascending order.

Sometimes a very small change in an algorithm will improve it immensely. The most commonly used replacement sort, which is the simple replacement sort found in many books and articles, is incredibly slow. This improved version delays the switch between two items until that item is found to be the smallest. This small modification halves the sorting time of the simple replacement sort.

Even though this sort is significantly faster than its close cousin mentioned above, it fails in one important respect: As the number of items to be sorted increases linearly, the time it takes to sort the items increases exponentially.

REFERENCE:

John P. Grillo, "A Comparison of Sorts," *Creative Computing*, Nov.–Dec. 1976, pp. 76–80.

LISTING:

```
1000 ' **** delayed replacement sort
1010 FOR I8=1 TO N-1
1020    K8=I8
1030    FOR J8=I8+1 TO N
1040       IF X(J8)<X(K8)
             THEN K8=J8
1050    NEXT J8
1060    IF I8<>K8
          THEN T8=X(K8) :
               X(K8)=X(I8) :
               X(I8)=T8
1070 NEXT I8
1080 RETURN
```

VARIABLES:

```
entering

    X:  List of values to be sorted
    N:  Number of values in X


exiting

    X:  Sorted list of values


local

    I8:  Outer loop index
    J8:  Inner loop index
    K8:  Indicator. If K8<>I8 then switch X(K8) and
         X(I8)
    T8:  Temporary holder during switch
```

NOTES

If TRS-80 BASIC had a SWAP command as do a few other BASICs, line 1060 could be written as

```
1060 IF I8<>K8 THEN SWAP X(I8), X(K8)
```

Compare this sort to the other three in Volume 1 of Subroutine Sandwich, and with the next two subroutines. You will be surprised at how the selection of an algorithm can improve the performance of a program.

PROGRAM LISTING:

```
10 ' program : delayed replacement sort : SS2TM1
20 ' authors : JOHN P GRILLO & JD ROBERTSON
30 '
40 DIM X(60)
50 RANDOM
60 PRINT "unsorted table"
70 N=10+RND(50)
80 FOR I=1 TO N
90    X(I)=9+RND(90)
100   IF I-INT(I/8)*8=1 THEN PRINT
110   PRINT USING "####";X(I);
120 NEXT I
130 GOSUB 1000   ' <<<< call delayed replacement sort
140 PRINT : PRINT : PRINT
150 PRINT "sorted table"
160 FOR I=1 TO N
170   IF I-INT(I/8)*8=1 THEN PRINT
180   PRINT USING "####";X(I);
190 NEXT I
200 STOP
1000 ' **** delayed replacement sort
1010 FOR I8=1 TO N-1
1020    K8=I8
1030    FOR J8=I8+1 TO N
1040       IF X(J8)<X(K8)
             THEN K8=J8
1050    NEXT J8
1060    IF I8<>K8
          THEN T8=X(K8) :
               X(K8)=X(I8) :
               X(I8)=T8
1070 NEXT I8
1080 RETURN
9999 END
```

RUN:

```
unsorted table

  49  58  32  67  23  63  41  97
  19  83  21  17  22  10  63  50
  10  79  48  93  87  83  87  92
  54  99  37  31  36  20  69  89
  12  53  50  41

sorted table

  10  10  12  17  19  20  21  22
  23  31  32  36  37  41  41  48
  49  50  50  53  54  58  63  63
  67  69  79  83  83  87  87  89
  92  93  97  99


unsorted table

  54  86  75  99  46  88  25  82
  38  68  54  94  64  48  34  37
  22  87  97  34  36  69  91  79
  78  91  88  90  22  26  63  52
  23  49  92  36  78  61  70  15
  94  85  46  20  28  91  78  99
  94  77  70  62  48  31


sorted table

  15  20  22  22  23  25  26  28
  31  34  34  36  36  37  38  46
  46  48  48  49  52  54  54  61
  62  63  64  68  69  70  70  75
  77  78  78  78  79  82  85  86
  87  88  88  90  91  91  91  92
  94  94  94  97  99  99
```

Subroutine: Insertion Sort SS2TM2

PURPOSE:

Arrange a list of values into ascending order.

The insertion sort is a surprise. It is relatively easy to code and understand, yet it is fast. Usually, fast sorting algorithms are difficult to understand. As this sort proceeds, each unsorted item is inserted in its appropriate spot relative to the other items already sorted. For example, the unsorted list 84735 would look like this after each successive iteration: 48735 47835 34785 34578. When the entire list has been scanned, the list is sorted. This sort is sometimes called the card player's sort.

REFERENCE:

Donald Knuth, "Sorting and Searching," *The Art of Computer Programming*, Vol. 3 (Reading, MA.: Addison-Wesley, 1973).

LISTING:

```
1000 ' **** insertion sort
1010 FOR I8=1 TO N-1
1020    K8=X(I8+1)
1030    FOR J8=I8 TO 1 STEP -1
1040       IF K8>=X(J8) THEN 1080
1050       X(J8+1)=X(J8)
1060    NEXT J8
1070    J8=0
1080    X(J8+1)=K8
1090 NEXT I8
1100 RETURN
```

VARIABLES:

```
entering

    X:  List of values to be sorted
    N:  Number of values in X


exiting

    X:  Sorted list of values


local

    I8:  External loop index
    J8:  Internal loop index
    K8:  First value in unsorted list
```

NOTES:

The outer loop, 1010–1090, defines K8 as the next item to be compared. The inner loop, 1030 to 1060, scans the sorted list from the bottom up to find the place where K8 must be inserted. When its proper location is found, it is inserted in the list. Notice that the inner loop expands the sorted list downward one position until the insertion position is found.

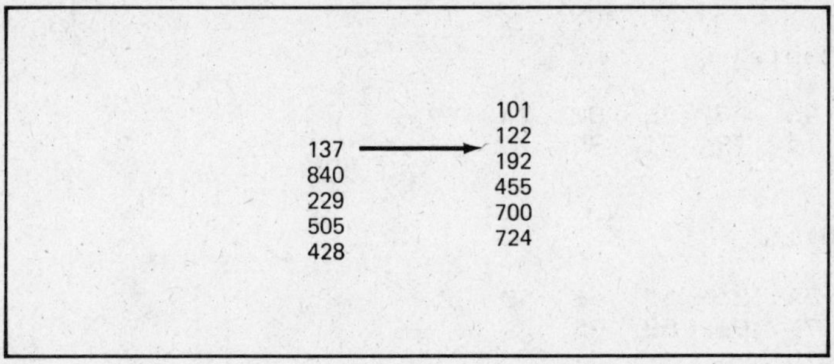

PROGRAM LISTING:

```
10 ' program : insertion sort : SS2TM2
20 ' authors : JOHN P GRILLO & JD ROBERTSON
30 '
40 DIM X(60)
50 RANDOM
60 PRINT "unsorted table"
70 N=10+RND(50)
80 FOR I=1 TO N
90    X(I)=9+RND(90)
100   IF I-INT(I/8)*8=1 THEN PRINT
110   PRINT USING "####";X(I);
120 NEXT I
130 GOSUB 1000    ' <<<< call insertion sort
140 PRINT : PRINT : PRINT
150 PRINT "sorted table"
160 FOR I=1 TO N
170    IF I-INT(I/8)*8=1 THEN PRINT
180    PRINT USING "####";X(I);
190 NEXT I
200 STOP
1000 ' **** insertion sort
1010 FOR I8=1 TO N-1
1020    K8=X(I8+1)
1030    FOR J8=I8 TO 1 STEP -1
1040       IF K8>=X(J8) THEN 1080
1050       X(J8+1)=X(J8)
1060    NEXT J8
1070    J8=0
1080    X(J8+1)=K8
1090 NEXT I8
1100 RETURN
9999 END
```

RUN:

```
unsorted table

  79  50  46  43  36  88  74  29
  11  34  55  79  81  95


sorted table

  11  29  34  36  43  46  50  55
  74  79  79  81  88  95
```

RUN (CONTINUED):

```
unsorted table

   30  25  11  72  40  69  82  52
   30  97  52  31  80  17  74  82
   75  42  52  12  33  19  97  35
   69  84  64  61  48  41  60  55
   37  58

sorted table

   11  12  17  19  25  30  30  31
   33  35  37  40  41  42  48  52
   52  52  55  58  60  61  64  69
   69  72  74  75  80  82  82  84
   97  97

unsorted table

   76  48  62  76  53  37  81  40
   97  62  15  49  86  38  11  12
   27  96  65  31  96  92  46  36
   20  70  63  15  64  86  83  45
   10  92  75  37  91  72  34  80
   23  58  74  45  74  44  53  70

sorted table

   10  11  12  15  15  20  23  27
   31  34  36  37  37  38  40  44
   45  45  46  48  49  53  53  58
   62  62  63  64  65  70  70  72
   74  74  75  76  76  80  81  83
   86  86  91  92  92  96  96  97
```

Subroutine: Quicksort SS2TM3

PURPOSE:

Arrange a list into ascending order.

The Quicksort is one of the very fastest sorting techniques. However, it suffers two disadvantages. First, it is complex and rather difficult to understand. Second, it must be programmed using a stack to hold a series of pointers unless the language you are using supports recursive programming.

REFERENCE:

Donald Knuth, "Sorting and Searching," *The Art of Computer Programming*, Vol. 3 (Reading, MA.: Addison-Wesley, 1973).

LISTING:

```
1000 ' **** Quicksort
1010 K8=0 : I8=0
1020 S(I8+1)=1 : S(I8+2)=N
1030 K8=K8+1
1040 IF K8=0 THEN RETURN
1050 K8=K8-1 : I8=K8+K8
1060 A8=S(I8+1) : B8=S(I8+2)
1070 Z8=X(A8) : U8=A8 : L8=B8+1
1080 L8=L8-1
1090 IF L8=U8 THEN 1140
1100 IF Z8<=X(L8)
        THEN 1080
        ELSE X(U8)=X(L8)
1110 U8=U8+1
1120 IF L8=U8 THEN 1140
1130 IF Z8>=X(U8)
        THEN 1110
        ELSE X(L8)=X(U8) : GOTO 1080
1140 X(U8)=Z8
1150 IF B8-U8>=2
        THEN I8=K8+K8 : S(I8+1)=U8+1 :
             S(I8+2)=B8 : K8=K8+1
1160 IF L8-A8>=2
        THEN I8=K8+K8 : S(I8+1)=A8 :
             S(I8+2)=L8-1 : K8=K8+1
1170 GOTO 1040
```

VARIABLES:

```
entering

    X:   List of values to be sorted
    S:   Stack to hold pointers to the list
    N:   Number of values of X

exiting

    X:   Sorted list of values

local

    K8:      Indicator. When zero, the sort is finished
    I8:      Stack pointer. I8+1 points to top of
             segment, I8+2 to bottom of segment
    A8, B8:  Values at top and bottom of segment
    U8, L8:  Pointers to top and bottom of segment
    Z8:      Value being compared against X(L8)
```

NOTES:

What a can of worms! We won't even pretend to clarify the way this sort works. You should work your way through the Knuth reference or some other good article or book on sorting if you really want to understand this sort. We maintain that if you don't know how a procedure works, but you know that is works, that shouldn't deter you from using it. So here it is. Use it and compare it with others, and we're sure that you'll find it useful.

The word Quicksort is always one word and always capitalized. This algorithm is at the core of every good commercial sort, including those found in other languages such as COBOL. We consider it the best choice with large lists if adequate memory is available.

PROGRAM LISTING:

```
10 ' program : Quicksort : SS2TM3
20 ' authors : JOHN P GRILLO & JD ROBERTSON
30 '
40 DIM X(60),S(40)
50 RANDOM
60 PRINT "unsorted table"
70 N=10+RND(50)
80 FOR I=1 TO N
90     X(I)=9+RND(90)
100    IF I-INT(I/8)*8=1 THEN PRINT
110    PRINT USING "####";X(I);
120 NEXT I
130 GOSUB 1000    ' <<<< call Quicksort
140 PRINT : PRINT : PRINT
150 PRINT "sorted table"
160 FOR I=1 TO N
170    IF I-INT(I/8)*8=1 THEN PRINT
180    PRINT USING "####";X(I);
190 NEXT I
200 STOP
1000 ' **** Quicksort
1010 K8=0 : I8=0
1020 S(I8+1)=1 : S(I8+2)=N
1030 K8=K8+1
1040 IF K8=0 THEN RETURN
1050 K8=K8-1 : I8=K8+K8
1060 A8=S(I8+1) : B8=S(I8+2)
1070 Z8=X(A8) : U8=A8 : L8=B8+1
1080 L8=L8-1
1090 IF L8=U8 THEN 1140
1100 IF Z8<=X(L8)
       THEN 1080
       ELSE X(U8)=X(L8)
1110 U8=U8+1
1120 IF L8=U8 THEN 1140
1130 IF Z8>=X(U8)
       THEN 1110
       ELSE X(L8)=X(U8) : GOTO 1080
1140 X(U8)=Z8
1150 IF B8-U8>=2
       THEN I8=K8+K8 : S(I8+1)=U8+1 :
            S(I8+2)=B8 : K8=K8+1
1160 IF L8-A8>=2
       THEN I8=K8+K8 : S(I8+1)=A8 :
            S(I8+2)=L8-1 : K8=K8+1
1170 GOTO 1040
9999 END
```

RUN:

```
unsorted table

  88  68  58  98  68  39  54  71
  35  71  91  84  81  17  14  47
  41  65  41

sorted table

  14  17  35  39  41  41  47  54
  58  65  68  68  71  71  81  84
  88  91  98

unsorted table

  24  13  31  52  24  30  99  84
  22  44  25  42  32  57  71  11
  79  29  98  45  21  22  97  75
  70  56  72  61  35  27  73  38
  64  55  40  49  23  87  57  51
  12  23  58  72  61  79

sorted table

  11  12  13  21  22  22  23  23
  24  24  25  27  29  30  31  32
  35  38  40  42  44  45  49  51
  52  55  56  57  57  58  61  61
  64  70  71  72  72  73  75  79
  79  84  87  97  98  99

unsorted table

  16  63  13  28  84  67  28  14
  26  84  97  59  91  86  61  62

sorted table

  13  14  16  26  28  28  59  61
  62  63  67  84  84  86  91  97
```

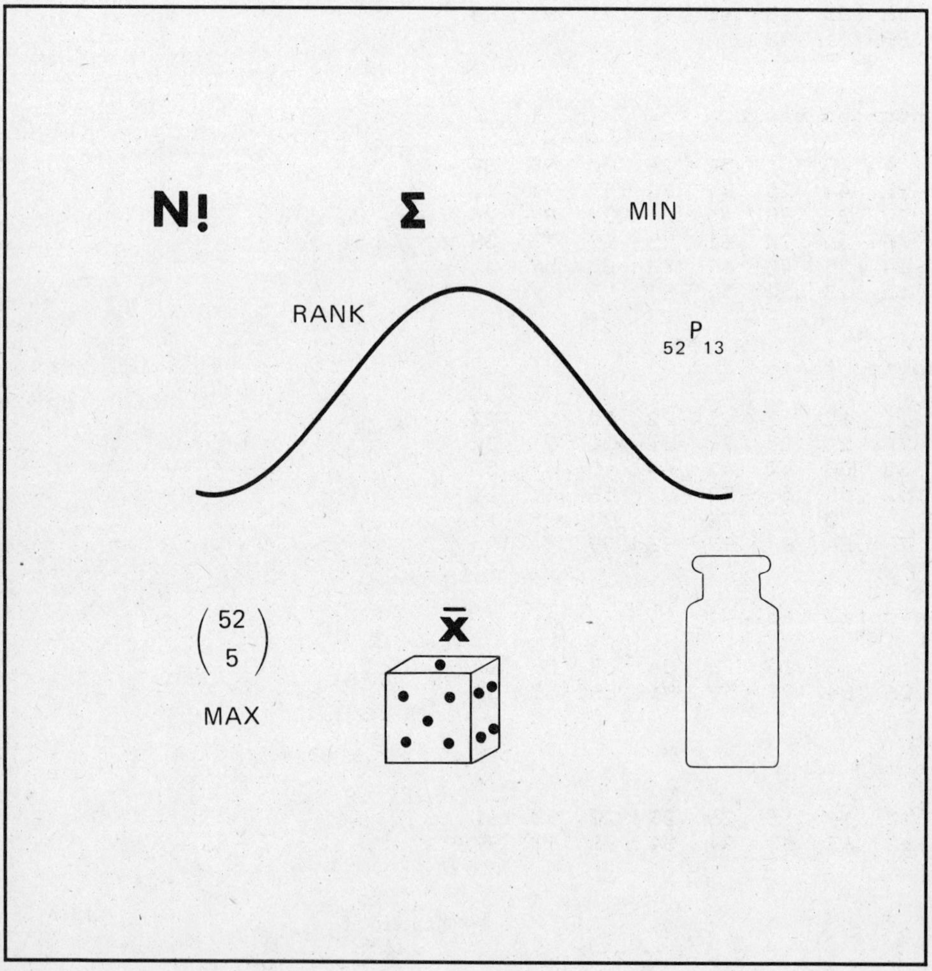
N!
Σ
MIN
RANK
$_{52}P_{13}$
$\binom{52}{5}$
MAX
$\bar{x}$

CHAPTER

8

$$\sum_{i=1}^{n}$$

STATISTICS

Introduction

We have included nine subroutines in the category of statistics, not because we are enamored of the subject but because the field uses so many easily computerized routines. In education, in the natural and social sciences, and in business, statistics has become an appropriate tool for data reduction.

The routines we have chosen to include here are found in many other books as well, indicating their popularity and their heavy use. Of particular note is Stirling's approximation, which in one calculation produces a value that is normally derived from a looping routine. The value returned is an approximation, but it is so close when the factorial is large that it is as good as the actual value for all intents and purposes.

The unit data normalization is a maximum-value-of-1 data transformation routine that contrasts with the first data normalization routine in the first book, Subroutine Sandwich. That routine was a sum-value-of-1 data transformation.

Subroutine: Rank SS2ST1

PURPOSE:

Generate the rank of each item in a list.

This subroutine assumes that two lists are supplied by the user. One list holds the values on which the ranks are based; the other list will hold the rankings once the subroutine calculates them.

REFERENCE:

Murray Spiegel, *Theory and Problems of Statistics*, Schaum's Outline Series (New York: McGraw-Hill, 1961), p. 246. This reference discusses a common use of ranked lists in determining rank order correlation.

LISTING:

```
1000 ' **** rank
1010 GOSUB 2000    ' <<<< call insertion sort
1020 Y(1)=1
1030 FOR I8=2 TO N
1040     IF X(I8)=X(I8-1)
            THEN Y(I8)=Y(I8-1)
            ELSE Y(I8)=I8
1050 NEXT I8
1060 RETURN
```

VARIABLES:

```
entering

   X:   List to be ranked
   Y:   List for ranks
   N:   Number of values in X

exiting

   X:   Original list to be ranked, in sorted order
   Y:   List of ranks

local

   I8:   Loop index
```

NOTES:

The subroutine calls another to sort the X array of values. This may be hazardous to the general welfare of your program, since X will be rearranged in memory as a result. The insertion sort is used, although any in-place sort would work also.

The primary function that this subroutine performs is to generate the set of ranks, based on the sorted X array. This is done by assigning the first rank as 1 (line 1020), then increasing the rank for each different value encountered in X. If the values are equal, so are their ranks.

PROGRAM LISTING:

```
10 ' program : rank : SS2ST1
20 ' authors : JOHN P GRILLO & JD ROBERTSON
30 '
40 DIM X(60),Y(60)
50 RANDOM
60 PRINT "data"
70 N=10+RND(50)
80 FOR I=1 TO N
90    X(I)=9+RND(90)
100   IF I-INT(I/8)*8=1 THEN PRINT
110   PRINT USING "####";X(I);
120 NEXT I
130 GOSUB 1000    ' <<<< call rank
140 PRINT : PRINT
150 PRINT "position ","data","rank"
160 FOR I=1 TO N
170    PRINT "  ";I;TAB(16);X(I);TAB(32);Y(I)
180 NEXT I
190 STOP
1000 ' **** rank
1010 GOSUB 2000    ' <<<< call insertion sort
1020 Y(1)=1
1030 FOR I8=2 TO N
1040    IF X(I8)=X(I8-1)
          THEN Y(I8)=Y(I8-1)
          ELSE Y(I8)=I8
1050 NEXT I8
1060 RETURN
2000 ' #### insertion sort
2010 FOR I8=1 TO N-1
2020    K8=X(I8+1)
2030    FOR J8=I8 TO 1 STEP -1
2040       IF K8>=X(J8) THEN 2080
2050       X(J8+1)=X(J8)
2060    NEXT J8
2070    J8=0
2080    X(J8+1)=K8
2090 NEXT I8
2100 RETURN
9999 END
```

RUN:

```
data

  50  51  62  52  27  33  54  96
  64  52  34  34  50  57  61  76
  56  47  34  89  47  10  59  53
  21  24  61  92  37  64  45  34
  38  58

position          data              rank
   1               10                1
   2               21                2
   3               24                3
   4               27                4
   5               33                5
   6               34                6
   7               34                6
   8               34                6
   9               34                6
  10               37               10
  11               38               11
  12               45               12
  13               47               13
  14               47               13
  15               50               15
  16               50               15
  17               51               17
  18               52               18
  19               52               18
  20               53               20
  21               54               21
  22               56               22
  23               57               23
  24               58               24
  25               59               25
  26               61               26
  27               61               26
  28               62               28
  29               64               29
  30               64               29
  31               76               31
  32               89               32
  33               92               33
  34               96               34
```

Subroutine: Minimum SS2ST2

PURPOSE:

Find the minimum value in a list.

The minimum value in a list is the list's smallest value. It is useful when determining the range of a set of values.

REFERENCE:

James Popham, *Educational Statistics* (New York: Harper & Row, 1967), p. 16.

LISTING:

```
1000 ' **** minimum
1010 M=X(1)
1020 FOR I8=2 TO N
1030    IF M>X(I8)
          THEN M=X(I8)
1040 NEXT I8
1050 RETURN
```

VARIABLES:

entering

X: List of values
N: Size of list X

exiting

M: Smallest, or minimum, value in X

local

I8: Loop index

NOTES:

Initially, the subroutine assumes in line 1010 that the first value X(1) is the minimum. The rest of the list is scanned starting at the second position. If a value smaller than the current minimum M is found, that value is assigned to M. Thus when the bottom of the list is reached, M contains the smallest value.

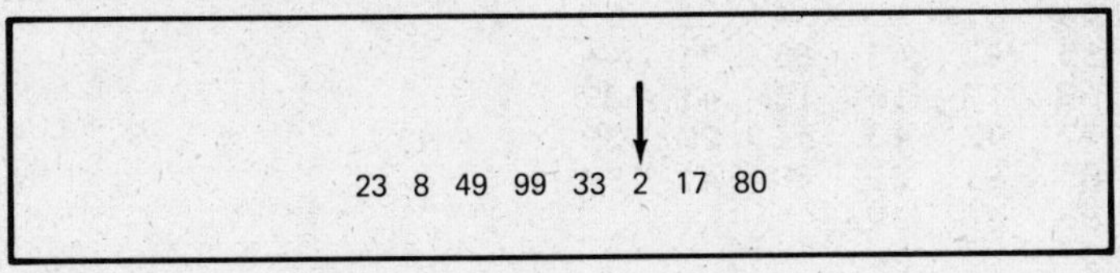

PROGRAM LISTING:

```
10 ' program : minimum : SS2ST2
20 ' authors : JOHN P GRILLO & JD ROBERTSON
30 '
40 DIM X(60)
50 RANDOM
60 PRINT "data"
70 N=10+RND(50)
80 FOR I=1 TO N
90    X(I)=9+RND(90)
100   IF I-INT(I/8)*8=1 THEN PRINT
110   PRINT USING "####";X(I);
120 NEXT I
130 GOSUB 1000    ' <<<< call minimum
140 PRINT : PRINT
150 PRINT "minimum",M
160 STOP
1000 ' **** minimum
1010 M=X(1)
1020 FOR I8=2 TO N
1030    IF M>X(I8)
          THEN M=X(I8)
1040 NEXT I8
1050 RETURN
9999 END
```

RUN:

```
data

  78  16  30  41  50  75  72  53
  83  80  14  62  93  64  22  53
  77  35  95  42  43  85  71  46
  89  30  60  17  16  15  41  39
  85  18  72  42  43  52  20  38
  14  74  85  61  22  49  41  90
  30  83  68  36  39

minimum        14
```

RUN (CONTINUED):

```
data

  27  76  19  13  62  57  32  31
  17  28  63  31  53  82  25  28
  50  65  81

minimum          13

data

  12  40  89  72  12  48  71  97
  73  42  22  72  76  19  89  19
  84  15  42  43  27

minimum          12

data

  61  76  94  11  25  52  38  50
  21  27  63  83  81  64  99  93

minimum          11

data

  23  42  46  60  78  60  92  19
  99  61  91

minimum          19

data

  78  78  40  42  97  33  11  75
  10  30  54  25  63  25  85  98
  99  48  88  92  28  45  35  85
  87  58  46  13  91  20  74

minimum          10
```

Subroutine: Maximum SS2ST3

PURPOSE:

Find the largest value in a list of values.

Together with the preceding subroutine SS2ST2, both the maximum and minimum are used to find the range of a list of values.

REFERENCE:

James Popham, *Educational Statistics* (New York: Harper & Row, 1967), p. 16.

LISTING:

```
1000 ' **** maximum
1010 M=X(1)
1020 FOR I8=2 TO N
1030    IF M<X(I8)
          THEN M=X(I8)
1040 NEXT I8
1050 RETURN
```

VARIABLES:

entering

X: List of values
N: Number of values in X

exiting

M: Largest, or maximum, value in X

local

I8: Loop index

NOTES:

This subroutine works in a similar fashion to the previous one. It assumes that the first value in the list is the largest one, then it scans the rest of the list. When it encounters a larger value than the one presently in M, it redefines M as that new high value.

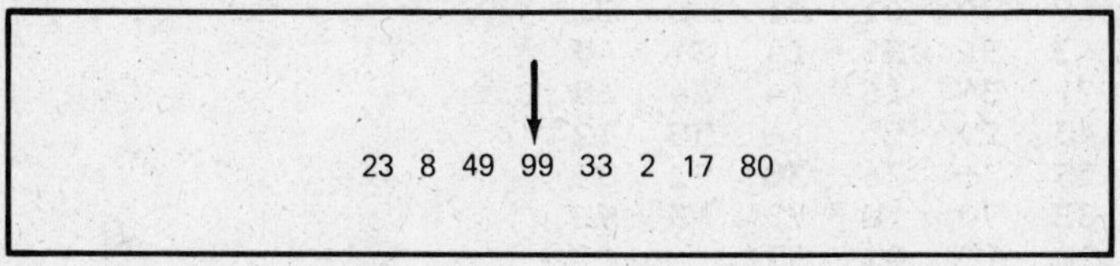

PROGRAM LISTING:

```
10 ' program : maximum : SS2ST3
20 ' authors : JOHN P GRILLO & JD ROBERTSON
30 '
40 DIM X(60)
50 RANDOM
60 PRINT "data"
70 N=10+RND(50)
80 FOR I=1 TO N
90    X(I)=9+RND(90)
100   IF I-INT(I/8)*8=1 THEN PRINT
110   PRINT USING "####";X(I);
120 NEXT I
130 GOSUB 1000    ' <<<< call maximum
140 PRINT : PRINT
150 PRINT "maximum",M
160 STOP
1000 ' **** maximum
1010 M=X(1)
1020 FOR I8=2 TO N
1030    IF M<X(I8)
          THEN M=X(I8)
1040 NEXT I8
1050 RETURN
9999 END
```

RUN:

```
data

  14  34  69  79  61  81  66  86
  27  42  43  91  31  14  31  40
  80  48  72  38  16  14  66  65
  71  66  43  29  55  16  58  72
  38  28  59  36  36  30  92  83
  22  99  38  30  10  97  43  98
  25  98  26  26  51  69

maximum        99
```

RUN (CONTINUED):

```
data

  19  37  68  21  26  45  58  38
  45  32  23  82  62  41  39  70
  88  93  53  29  49  43  35  77
  18  37  15  10  62  52  10  49

maximum          93

data

  35  28  62  59  51  77  86  95
  65  97  88  48  26  20  45  49
  35  41  36  89  13  54  36  69
  73  47  49  95  55  28  43  36

maximum          97

data

  67  83  10  58  24  98  37  88
  75  66  49  40  51  72  73  47
  83  19  28  53  33  56  48  89
  71  79  57  87  61  27

maximum          98

data

  55  21  64  42  49  78  35  28
  84  73  33  96  48  14  52  37
  45  61  72

maximum          96

data

  66  39  26  72  49  42  32  73
  90  80  20  63  82  65  40  72

maximum          90
```

Subroutine: Stirling's Approximation SS2ST4

PURPOSE:

Calculate the log of X factorial.

The calling program supplies an integer, and the subroutine returns the natural log of the factorial of that integer. For example, if the integer X is 7, X! is $7 \times 6 \times 5 \times 4 \times 3 \times 2 \times 1$, which is 5040. The natural log of 5040 is, to 6 significant digits, 8.52517. This last number is what the Stirling approximation subroutine returns.

This subroutine is particularly useful in statistical applications, specifically for calculating probabilities, combinations, and permutations.

REFERENCE:

Charles Hodgman, Ed., *Handbook of Chemistry and Physics* (Cleveland: Chemical Rubber Publishing, 1956), p. 303.

LISTING:

```
1000 ' **** Stirling's approximation
1010 S=1
1020 IF X<=0
       THEN S=0 : RETURN
1030 FOR I8=1 TO 10
1040    S=S*I8
1050    IF X=I8
          THEN S=LOG(S) : RETURN
1060 NEXT I8
1070 S=LOG(6.283186)/2+LOG(X)*(X+0.5)-X+1/(12*X)
1080 RETURN
```

VARIABLES:

```
entering

   X:   Integer for which factorial is desired

exiting

   S:   Stirling's approximation of log of X!

local

   I8:  Loop index for factorial up to 10!
```

NOTES:

If X is 10 or less, the exact log of X! is returned. If X is greater than 10, the approximation of log of X! is returned using Stirling's formula.

1 X 2 X 3 X 4 X . . . . = !

PROGRAM LISTING:

```
10 ' program : Stirling's approximation : SS2ST4
20 ' authors : JOHN P GRILLO & JD ROBERTSON
30 '
40 PRINT
50 INPUT "input integer for which factorial is desired";X
60 IF X<0 THEN STOP
70 GOSUB 1000    ' <<<< call Stirling's approximation
80 PRINT
90 PRINT "log of";X;"factorial is approximately";S
100 IF X<34
     THEN PRINT X;"factorial is approximately";INT(EXP(S)+0.5)
110 GOTO 40
1000 ' **** Stirling's approximation
1010 S=1
1020 IF X<=0
       THEN S=0 : RETURN
1030 FOR I8=1 TO 10
1040    S=S*I8
1050    IF X=I8
          THEN S=LOG(S) : RETURN
1060 NEXT I8
1070 S=LOG(6.283186)/2+LOG(X)*(X+0.5)-X+1/(12*X)
1080 RETURN
9999 END
```

RUN:

```
input integer for which factorial is desired? 1

log of 1 factorial is approximately 0
 1 factorial is approximately 1

input integer for which factorial is desired? 2

log of 2 factorial is approximately .693147
 2 factorial is approximately 2

input integer for which factorial is desired? 3

log of 3 factorial is approximately 1.79176
 3 factorial is approximately 6

input integer for which factorial is desired? 4

log of 4 factorial is approximately 3.17805
 4 factorial is approximately 24
```

RUN (CONTINUED):

```
input integer for which factorial is desired? 5

log of 5 factorial is approximately 4.78749
 5 factorial is approximately 120

input integer for which factorial is desired? 6

log of 6 factorial is approximately 6.57925
 6 factorial is approximately 720

input integer for which factorial is desired? 7

log of 7 factorial is approximately 8.52516
 7 factorial is approximately 5040

input integer for which factorial is desired? 8

log of 8 factorial is approximately 10.6046
 8 factorial is approximately 40320

input integer for which factorial is desired? 9

log of 9 factorial is approximately 12.8018
 9 factorial is approximately 362880

input integer for which factorial is desired? 10

log of 10 factorial is approximately 15.1044
 10 factorial is approximately 3.6288E+06

input integer for which factorial is desired? 52

log of 52 factorial is approximately 156.361

input integer for which factorial is desired? 13

log of 13 factorial is approximately 22.5522
 13 factorial is approximately 6.22704E+09

input integer for which factorial is desired? 0

log of 0 factorial is approximately 0
 0 factorial is approximately 1
```

Subroutine: Combinations SS2ST5

PURPOSE:

Calculate combination of N things taken M at a time.

This subroutine answers such questions as "How many different 5-card poker hands exist?" or "How many ways can a 3-car garage be filled given 10 different cars?" The calculation relies on the use of factorials, which in this case are produced using another subroutine, Stirling's approximation.

REFERENCE:

J. E. Freund and F. J. Williams, *Elementary Business Statistics: The Modern Approach* (Englewood Cliffs, NJ: Prentice-Hall, 1977), p. 92.

LISTING:

```
1000 ' **** combinations
1010 X=N
1020 GOSUB 2000    ' <<<< call Stirling's approximation
1030 N8=S
1040 X=M
1050 GOSUB 2000    ' <<<< call Stirling's approximation
1060 M8=S
1070 X=N-M
1080 GOSUB 2000    ' <<<< call Stirling's approximation
1090 D8=S
1100 C=INT(EXP(N8-(M8+D8))+0.5)
1110 RETURN
```

VARIABLES:

entering

N: Number of things, for example 52 cards
M: Taken M at a time, for example 5 per hand

exiting

C: Combination of N things taken M at a time

local

N8: Log of N factorial (N!)
M8: Log of M factorial (M!)
D8: Log of (N-M) factorial (N-M)!

NOTES:

Most of the work of this subroutine is done in the Stirling's approximation subroutine SS2ST4, which calculates the logs of the factorials needed. This subroutine calculates C in line 1100 by rounding the exponential value returned to the nearest integer. The formula, using integers, would be N!/(M!*(N-M)!). Using logs, this formula can be expressed as exp(log(N!)–(log(M!)+log(N–M)!). Since Stirling's approximation produces the log of a factorial, this subroutine's work is fairly simple.

$$\binom{N}{M} = {}_{N}C_{M} = \frac{N!}{M!(N-M)!}$$

PROGRAM LISTING:

```
10 ' program : combinations : SS2ST5
20 ' authors : JOHN P GRILLO & JD ROBERTSON
30 '
40 PRINT
50 INPUT "how many 'things'";N
60 IF N<=0 THEN STOP
70 INPUT "how many 'at a time'";M
80 GOSUB 1000    ' <<<< call combinations
90 PRINT
100 PRINT "combinations of";N;"things taken";M;"at a time is";C
110 GOTO 40
1000 ' **** combinations
1010 X=N
1020 GOSUB 2000    ' <<<< call Stirling's approximation
1030 N8=S
1040 X=M
1050 GOSUB 2000    ' <<<< call Stirling's approximation
1060 M8=S
1070 X=N-M
1080 GOSUB 2000    ' <<<< call Stirling's approximation
1090 D8=S
1100 C=INT(EXP(N8-(M8+D8))+0.5)
1110 RETURN
2000 ' #### Stirling's approximation
2010 S=1
2020 IF X<=0
       THEN S=0 : RETURN
2030 FOR I8=1 TO 10
2040    S=S*I8
2050    IF X=I8
          THEN S=LOG(S) : RETURN
2060 NEXT I8
2070 S=LOG(6.283186)/2+LOG(X)*(X+0.5)-X+1/(12*X)
2080 RETURN
9999 END
```

RUN:

```
how many 'things'? 6
how many 'at a time'? 0

combinations of 6 things taken 0 at a time is 1

how many 'things'? 6
how many 'at a time'? 1

combinations of 6 things taken 1 at a time is 6

how many 'things'? 6
how many 'at a time'? 2

combinations of 6 things taken 2 at a time is 15

how many 'things'? 6
how many 'at a time'? 3

combinations of 6 things taken 3 at a time is 20

how many 'things'? 6
how many 'at a time'? 4

combinations of 6 things taken 4 at a time is 15

how many 'things'? 6
how many 'at a time'? 5

combinations of 6 things taken 5 at a time is 6

how many 'things'? 6
how many 'at a time'? 6

combinations of 6 things taken 6 at a time is 1

how many 'things'? 10
how many 'at a time'? 3

combinations of 10 things taken 3 at a time is 120

how many 'things'? 52
how many 'at a time'? 5

combinations of 52 things taken 5 at a time is 2.59894E+06
```

Subroutine: Permutations SS2ST6

PURPOSE:

Calculate the permutations of N things M at a time.

You can think of permutations as arrangements, whereas combinations were simple selections. For example, there are only 120 possible 3-card hands if you use a 10-card deck, but since there are six ways each hand can be arranged (A-K-Q, A-Q-K, K-A-Q, K-Q-A, Q-A-K, Q-K-A, for instance), there are 720 possible arrangements, or permutations, of 3-card hands in a 10-card deck.

Stirling's approximation is again useful in this subroutine for calculating the logs of the larger factorials.

REFERENCE:

J. E. Freund and F. J. Williams, *Elementary Business Statistics: The Modern Approach* (Englewood Cliffs, NJ, Prentice-Hall, 1977), p. 92.

LISTING:

```
1000 ' **** permutations
1010 X=N
1020 GOSUB 2000    ' <<<< call Stirling's approximation
1030 N8=S
1040 X=N-M
1050 GOSUB 2000    ' <<<< call Stirling's approximation
1060 M8=S
1070 P=INT(EXP(N8-M8)+0.5)
1080 RETURN
```

VARIABLES:

```
entering

   N:   Number of "things", for example 52 cards
   M:   Taken M at a time, for example 5 per hand


exiting

   P:   Permutations of N things taken M at a time


local

   N8:  Log of N factorial (N!)
   M8:  Log of (N-M) factorial (N-M)!
```

NOTES:

Permutations and combinations are used often in the calculation of probabilities of events in statistics.

This subroutine uses the formula P = N!/(N-M)!. Lines 1010–1030 calculate N8 as the log of N!, using the subroutine SS2ST4. Then lines 1040–1060 calculate M8 as the log of (N-M)!. Line 1070 produces the rounded integer form of P using the exponential function, as did the combinations subroutine.

$$ {}_{N}P_{M} = \frac{N!}{(N-M)!} $$

PROGRAM LISTING:

```
10 ' program : permutations : SS2ST6
20 ' authors : JOHN P GRILLO & JD ROBERTSON
30 '
40 PRINT
50 INPUT "how many 'things'";N
60 IF N<=0 THEN STOP
70 INPUT "how many 'at a time'";M
80 GOSUB 1000   ' <<<< call permutations
90 PRINT
100 PRINT "permutations of";N;"things taken";M;"at a time is";P
110 GOTO 40
1000 ' **** permutations
1010 X=N
1020 GOSUB 2000   ' <<<< call Stirling's approximation
1030 N8=S
1040 X=N-M
1050 GOSUB 2000   ' <<<< call Stirling's approximation
1060 M8=S
1070 P=INT(EXP(N8-M8)+0.5)
1080 RETURN
2000 ' #### Stirling's approximation
2010 S=1
2020 IF X<=0
       THEN S=0 : RETURN
2030 FOR I8=1 TO 10
2040    S=S*I8
2050    IF X=I8
          THEN S=LOG(S) : RETURN
2060 NEXT I8
2070 S=LOG(6.283186)/2+LOG(X)*(X+0.5)-X+1/(12*X)
2080 RETURN
9999 END
```

RUN:

```
how many 'things'? 6
how many 'at a time'? 0

permutations of 6 things taken 0 at a time is 1

how many 'things'? 6
how many 'at a time'? 1

permutations of 6 things taken 1 at a time is 6

how many 'things'? 6
how many 'at a time'? 2

permutations of 6 things taken 2 at a time is 30

how many 'things'? 6
how many 'at a time'? 3

permutations of 6 things taken 3 at a time is 120

how many 'things'? 6
how many 'at a time'? 4

permutations of 6 things taken 4 at a time is 360

how many 'things'? 6
how many 'at a time'? 5

permutations of 6 things taken 5 at a time is 720

how many 'things'? 6
how many 'at a time'? 6

permutations of 6 things taken 6 at a time is 720

how many 'things'? 10
how many 'at a time'? 3

permutations of 10 things taken 3 at a time is 720

how many 'things'? 52
how many 'at a time'? 5

permutations of 52 things taken 5 at a time is 3.11872E+08
```

Subroutine: Geometric Mean SS2ST7

PURPOSE:

Calculate the geometric mean of a sample.

The mean of a set of values is intended to be a measure of central tendency. That is, given a mean, you should be able to infer that it represents the data. Put another way, the mean is typical of the values. In most cases the arithmetic mean (the sum divided by the number of values) is sufficient. However, there are some types of values, such as ratios, percentages, rates of change, and index numbers in business applications, for which the arithmetic mean is inappropriate. The geometric mean is always less than the arithmetic mean.

In this subroutine, the calling program supplies a list of values and the number of values. The subroutine returns a single value, the geometric mean.

REFERENCE:

J. E. Freund and F. J. Williams, *Elementary Business Statistics: The Modern Approach* (Englewood Cliffs, NJ: Prentice-Hall, 1977), pp. 33 and 66.

LISTING:

```
1000 ' **** geometric mean
1010 S8=0
1020 FOR I8=1 TO N
1030     S8=S8+LOG(X(I8))
1040 NEXT I8
1050 G=EXP(S8/N)
1060 RETURN
```

VARIABLES:

```
entering

   X:   List of values
   N:   Number of values in X

exiting

   G:   Geometric mean

local

   S8:  Sum of the logs of X
   I8:  Loop index
```

NOTES:

To calculate a geometric mean, you can take the Nth root of the product of all X values, or you can add the logs of all X values and then take the antilog of that sum. The result is the same. We chose the second method because the product of even a short series of numbers exceeds the size of numbers representable by a computer.

$$\overline{G} = \left(\prod_{i=1}^{n} x_i \right)^{1/n}$$

PROGRAM LISTING:

```
10 ' program : geometric mean : SS2ST7
20 ' authors : JOHN P GRILLO & JD ROBERTSON
30 '
40 DIM X(60)
50 RANDOM
60 N=10+RND(50)
70 FOR I=1 TO N
80    X(I)=9+RND(90)
90 NEXT I
100 PRINT "data"
110 FOR I=1 TO N
120    IF I-INT(I/8)*8=1 THEN PRINT
130    PRINT USING "####";X(I);
140 NEXT I
150 GOSUB 1000    ' <<<< call geometric mean
160 PRINT : PRINT
170 PRINT "geometric mean",G
180 STOP
1000 ' **** geometric mean
1010 S8=0
1020 FOR I8=1 TO N
1030    S8=S8+LOG(X(I8))
1040 NEXT I8
1050 G=EXP(S8/N)
1060 RETURN
9999 END
```

RUN:

```
data

  77  88  38  48  72  67  62  87
  87  98  73  27  21  63  29  45
  81  16  22  97  24  87  98  77
  96  87  55  49  44

geometric mean   55.5903
```

RUN (CONTINUED):

```
data

  64  91  67  45  59  63  21  57
  43  76  11  99  86  59  93  65
  97  17  78  58  13  39  39  16
  78  93  74  48  93  82  43  19
  94  46  98  17  99  80  16  75
  18  42  45  53  80  55  96  34
  66  80  99  69  50  18

geometric mean    51.132

data

  50  36  44  12  98  31  19  14
  96  83  30  84  81  73  71  15
  74  35  26  58  43  40  76  31
  32  60  95  25  90  78  17  11
  84  88  88  51  24  70  99  38
  15  35  52  43  94  45  67  11
  40

geometric mean    43.8384

data

  25  30  94  64  58  13  46  45
  11  13  32  86  34  62  38  78
  80  91  48  69  48  33  86  35
  73  75  50  82  88  91  63  85
  69  24  87  23  89  86  48  25
  73  16  32  26

geometric mean    47.4475

data

  43  93  36  85  11  42  68  55
  11  27  19  28  35  30  85  61
  16  27  37  21  38  42  14  84
  81  10  17  41  93  58  28  25
  47  53  95  37  67  18  40  92
  71  81  38

geometric mean    38.794
```

Subroutine: Weighted Average SS2ST8

PURPOSE:

Calculate the weighted average of a sample.

A weighted average is useful in numerous applications. For example, in the calculation of student grades, each grade weighs a certain amount relative to all the others.

This subroutine accepts two lists from the calling program: A list of values and a list of weights for each value. The latter could be percentages, decimal values, or relative weights. The subroutine returns a single value, the weighted average.

REFERENCE:

J. E. Freund and F. J. Williams, *Elementary Business Statistics: The Modern Approach* (Englewood Cliffs, NJ: Prentice-Hall, 1977), p.31.

LISTING:

```
1000 ' **** weighted average
1010 S8=0 : W8=0
1020 FOR I8=1 TO N
1030     S8=S8+W(I8)*X(I8)
1040     W8=W8+W(I8)
1050 NEXT I8
1060 A=S8/W8
1070 RETURN
```

VARIABLES:

```
entering

    X:   List of values to be averaged
    W:   List of weights corresponding to each X
    N:   Number of values in X (and in W)

exiting

    A:   Weighted average

local

    S8:  Sum of products of value and weight
    W8:  Sum of weights
    I8:  Loop index
```

NOTES:

Line 1030 sums the products of values and weights into S8, and line 1040 sums the weights. Once both sums are calculated, the average is simply their quotient.

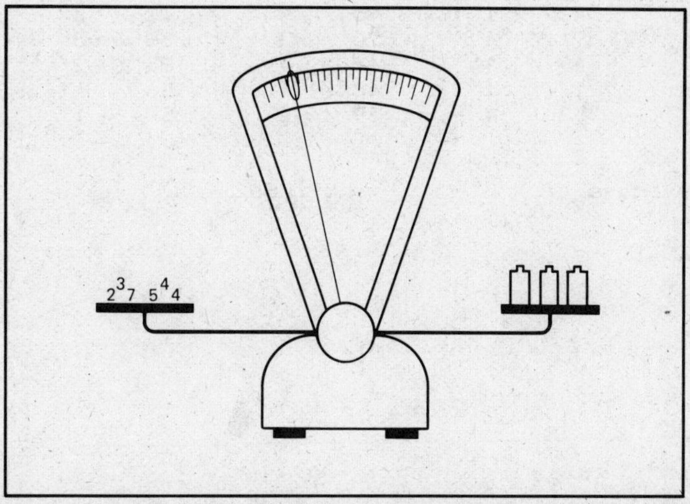

PROGRAM LISTING:

```
10 ' program : weighted average : SS2ST8
20 ' authors : JOHN P GRILLO & JD ROBERTSON
30 '
40 DIM X(60),W(60)
50 RANDOM
60 N=10+RND(50)
70 FOR I=1 TO N
80    X(I)=9+RND(90) : W(I)=RND(4)
90 NEXT I
100 PRINT "data / weights"
110 FOR I=1 TO N
120    IF I-INT(I/4)*4=1 THEN PRINT
130    PRINT USING "#### / ##      ";X(I),W(I);
140 NEXT I
150 GOSUB 1000    ' <<<< call weighted average
160 PRINT : PRINT
170 PRINT "weighted average",A
180 STOP
1000 ' **** weighted average
1010 S8=0 : W8=0
1020 FOR I8=1 TO N
1030    S8=S8+W(I8)*X(I8)
1040    W8=W8+W(I8)
1050 NEXT I8
1060 A=S8/W8
1070 RETURN
9999 END
```

RUN:

```
data / weights

  16 /  4       42 /  1       95 /  4       22 /  3
  48 /  1       91 /  4       70 /  3       38 /  3
  49 /  2       69 /  4       64 /  4       85 /  2
  63 /  2       17 /  1       48 /  4       56 /  4
  65 /  2       33 /  4       79 /  1       59 /  1
  95 /  4

weighted average             59.0862
```

RUN (CONTINUED):

```
data / weights

  45 /  4        56 /  2        76 /  3        41 /  4
  99 /  4        33 /  2        52 /  4        70 /  2
  46 /  3        96 /  3        22 /  4        60 /  1
  32 /  3        95 /  2        41 /  3        36 /  2
  61 /  2        87 /  2        94 /  4        29 /  3
  40 /  2        20 /  2        43 /  1        29 /  1
  91 /  3        49 /  1        38 /  3        29 /  4
  62 /  2        40 /  2        17 /  1        72 /  4
  19 /  3        67 /  3        26 /  1        26 /  4
  20 /  3        94 /  3        79 /  3        77 /  3
  70 /  3        23 /  4        29 /  2        56 /  2
  79 /  1        98 /  3        54 /  3        22 /  3
  84 /  1        48 /  2        83 /  3

weighted average                54.594

data / weights

  77 /  3        36 /  4        66 /  3        32 /  2
  81 /  2        81 /  3        36 /  1        25 /  3
  79 /  1        27 /  3        44 /  2        68 /  4
  64 /  1        44 /  2        70 /  4        21 /  4
  85 /  3        28 /  2        40 /  3        79 /  1
  21 /  3        12 /  1        45 /  3        99 /  1
  76 /  4        25 /  4        29 /  2        92 /  4

weighted average                52.5753

data / weights

  19 /  2        28 /  1        67 /  2        81 /  3
  28 /  2        42 /  4        22 /  4        99 /  2
  53 /  4        66 /  2        43 /  1        21 /  1
  99 /  1        35 /  2        49 /  4        48 /  2
  29 /  3        90 /  1        61 /  1        24 /  4
  58 /  1        82 /  1        72 /  4        23 /  4
  79 /  1        71 /  3        91 /  2        33 /  2
  70 /  3        99 /  2        95 /  4        93 /  4
  45 /  2        52 /  1        79 /  2        62 /  1
  11 /  1        70 /  4        98 /  1        33 /  2
  14 /  4        49 /  1        42 /  1        10 /  3
  92 /  4

weighted average                55.1731
```

Subroutine: Unit Data Normalization SS2ST9

PURPOSE:

Normalize or transform values to between 0 and 1.

We almost called this a plotting subroutine because of its immediate application to graphs and plots. Often you will have a set of data values to plot, and their values are scattered and don't conform easily to either the computer screen or the printed page. You are forced to change all values by a factor to make them fit.

This subroutine first finds the largest value in the set and changes it to 1. Then it proportions all the others to that one, forcing all values between 0 and 1. All values should be positive for this subroutine to yield meaningful results.

REFERENCE:

We created this procedure when the need arose in a graphing application.

LISTING:

```
1000 ' **** unit data normalization
1010 GOSUB 2000    ' <<<< call maximum
1020 FOR I8=1 TO N
1030     X(I8)=X(I8)/M
1040 NEXT I8
1050 RETURN
```

VARIABLES:

entering

X: List of values to be normalized
N: Number of values in X

exiting

X: Original list, now normalized

local

I8: Loop index
M: Maximum value in list X (from maximum subroutine)

NOTES:

Line 1010 calls the subroutine SS2ST3, described earlier in this chapter, to determine the largest value in X. Then the loop in lines 1020 through 1040 divide each successive value in X by that maximum, giving values between 0 and 1, which are proportional to the original values.

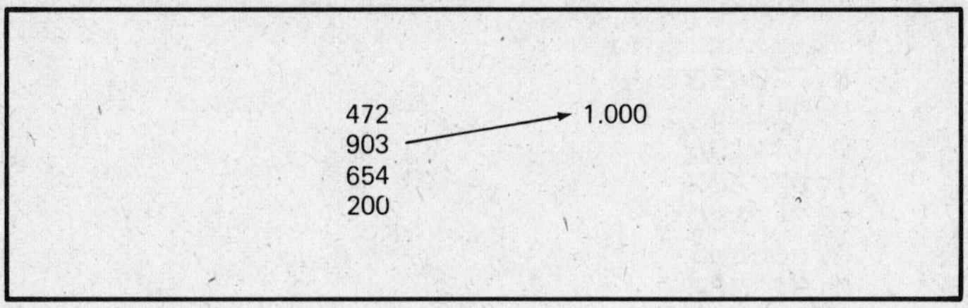

PROGRAM LISTING:

```
10 ' program : unit data normalization : SS2ST9
20 ' authors : JOHN P GRILLO & JD ROBERTSON
30 '
40 DIM X(12),Y(12)
50 RANDOM
60 N=4+RND(8)
70 FOR I=1 TO N
80    X(I)=100+RND(200)
90    Y(I)=X(I)
100 NEXT I
110 GOSUB 1000    ' <<<< call unit data normalization
120 PRINT " #   data   normalized data"
130 FOR I=1 TO N
140    PRINT USING "##    ###      #.######";I,Y(I),X(I)
150 NEXT I
160 STOP
1000 ' **** unit data normalization
1010 GOSUB 2000   ' <<<< call maximum
1020 FOR I8=1 TO N
1030    X(I8)=X(I8)/M
1040 NEXT I8
1050 RETURN
2000 ' #### maximum
2010 M=X(1)
2020 FOR I8=2 TO N
2030    IF M<X(I8)
          THEN M=X(I8)
2040 NEXT I8
2050 RETURN
9999 END
```

RUN:

```
 #   data   normalized data
 1    224      0.780488
 2    233      0.811847
 3    205      0.714286
 4    287      1.000000
 5    213      0.742160
 6    191      0.665505
 7    236      0.822300
 8    153      0.533101
 9    255      0.888502
10    184      0.641115
11    121      0.421603
```

RUN (CONTINUED):

#	data	normalized data
1	293	0.986532
2	184	0.619529
3	297	1.000000
4	178	0.599327
5	281	0.946128
6	171	0.575758

#	data	normalized data
1	142	0.494774
2	287	1.000000
3	190	0.662021
4	148	0.515679
5	132	0.459930
6	148	0.515679
7	104	0.362369

#	data	normalized data
1	225	0.845865
2	188	0.706767
3	262	0.984962
4	199	0.748120
5	150	0.563910
6	147	0.552632
7	160	0.601504
8	226	0.849624
9	266	1.000000
10	104	0.390977
11	234	0.879699

#	data	normalized data
1	293	1.000000
2	290	0.989761
3	202	0.689420
4	166	0.566553
5	252	0.860068
6	109	0.372014
7	114	0.389078
8	153	0.522184
9	281	0.959044

#	data	normalized data
1	183	0.620339
2	126	0.427119
3	198	0.671187
4	144	0.488136
5	109	0.369492
6	199	0.674576
7	204	0.691526
8	163	0.552542
9	241	0.816949
10	295	1.000000
11	238	0.806780
12	150	0.508475

CHAPTER

9

TABLE LOOKUP AND UTILITIES

Introduction

The operation called searching is performed to access an item from any list or table. It is a fundamental tool used to look up information in a file or in an array. People perform table lookups all the time—when reading a table of contents, an index, a glossary, a dictionary, or a phone book. These searches are conducted on lists that have some order. However, sometimes we search a magazine for an article or picture we remember having seen, and we only remember the relative page position and topic. This latter technique is a content- or topic-driven search rather than an order-driven search as in the former examples.

The utility routine we have included in this chapter is often used when an order that looks random is desired, yet there must be no repeats of the data items. For example, in card and dice games, in jury or committee selection, or in simulations, the elements themselves exist as distinct entities, yet their order must appear random.

Few programmers are aware of the power and speed of the Monte Carlo technique for shuffling cards. The usual shuffling scheme is to generate the 52 cards in order, then to pick one at random and place it into another table if it is not already there. It's this last phrase that's the catch, since that table search must be performed 51 times, and each time that search gets longer. The Monte Carlo shuffle is much faster and results in as good a distribution of cards.

Subroutine: Linear Unsorted Table Search SS2TL1

PURPOSE:

Search an unsorted table for a specific entry.

The calling program supplies a table (list) of numeric keys, each of which has associated with it a string entry in another table. You may think of these two lists as ID number and name, or part number and part description, or serial number and item description.

REFERENCE:

E. S. Page and L. B. Wilson, *Information Representation and Manipulation in a Computer*, 2nd ed. (New York: Cambridge University Press, 1978), p. 163.

LISTING:

```
1000 ' **** linear unsorted table search
1010 S=0
1020 FOR I8=1 TO N
1030     IF A=X(I8)
           THEN S=I8 : RETURN
1040 NEXT I8
1050 RETURN
```

VARIABLES:

```
entering

    X:   List of numeric keys
    N:   Number of keys in X
    A:   Search argument

exiting

    S:   Position (subscript) of A in X

local

    I8:  Loop index
```

NOTES:

This subroutine returns the position of the key in the list if it is found. If the key sought is not in X, the subroutine returns a zero in S, indicating an unsuccessful search.

A particular advantage of this searching technique is the fact that any new data element can be added to the bottom of the list without any rearrangement, and the search routine doesn't change. This technique could be useful for smaller lists. Be careful, though, because the number of comparisons (in line 1030) is on the average half the length of the list. This means that for longer lists the search could be very time-consuming.

PROGRAM LISTING:

```
10 ' program : linear unsorted table search : SS2TL1
20 ' authors : JOHN P GRILLO & JD ROBERTSON
30 '
40 CLEAR 1000
50 DIM X(10),X$(10)
60 PRINT
70 RESTORE
80 READ N
90 PRINT "element# - variety# / name;"
100 FOR I=1 TO N
110     READ X(I),X$(I)
120 NEXT I
130 W=2
140 GOSUB 2000    ' <<<< call columnar print routine
150 PRINT : PRINT
160 INPUT "input search argument (variety#)";A
170 IF A<0 THEN STOP
180 GOSUB 1000    ' <<<< call linear unsorted table search
190 PRINT
200 IF S=0
      THEN PRINT "linear search unsuccessful"
      ELSE PRINT X$(S)
210 GOTO 60
220 DATA 8 :    ' pumpkins
230 DATA 4,"big max",15,"big tom",5,"cinderella"
240 DATA 18,"jack-o'-lantern",11,"lady godiva",8,"small sugar"
250 DATA 17,"spirit hybrid",1,"triple treat"
260 STOP
1000 ' **** linear unsorted table search
1010 S=0
1020 FOR I8=1 TO N
1030    IF A=X(I8)
          THEN S=I8 : RETURN
1040 NEXT I8
1050 RETURN
2000 ' #### columnar print routine
2010 P8$="## - ## / %                   %"
2020 L8=INT((N-1)/W) : M8=L8+1 : N8=N-W*L8
2030 IF N=INT(N/W)*W
       THEN L8=L8+1 : S8=1
       ELSE S8=0
2040 FOR I8=1 TO L8
2050    K8=0
2060    FOR J8=1 TO W
2070       PRINT USING P8$;I8+K8;X(I8+K8);X$(I8+K8);
2080       IF J8>N8 THEN K8=K8+L8 ELSE K8=K8+M8
2090    NEXT J8
```

RUN:

```
2100 PRINT
2110 NEXT I8
2120 IF S8=1 THEN RETURN
2130 K8=0
2140 FOR J8=1 TO N8
2150    PRINT USING P8$;M8+K8;X(M8+K8);X$(M8+K8);
2160    K8=K8+M8
2170 NEXT J8
2180 PRINT
2190 RETURN
9999 END
```

```
element# - variety# / name;
 1 -  4 / big max            5 - 11 / lady godiva
 2 - 15 / big tom            6 -  8 / small sugar
 3 -  5 / cinderella         7 - 17 / spirit hybrid
 4 - 18 / jack-o'-lantern    8 -  1 / triple treat

input search argument (variety#)? 18

jack-o'-lantern

element# - variety# / name;
 1 -  4 / big max            5 - 11 / lady godiva
 2 - 15 / big tom            6 -  8 / small sugar
 3 -  5 / cinderella         7 - 17 / spirit hybrid
 4 - 18 / jack-o'-lantern    8 -  1 / triple treat

input search argument (variety#)? 16

linear search unsuccessful

element# - variety# / name;
 1 -  4 / big max            5 - 11 / lady godiva
 2 - 15 / big tom            6 -  8 / small sugar
 3 -  5 / cinderella         7 - 17 / spirit hybrid
 4 - 18 / jack-o'-lantern    8 -  1 / triple treat

input search argument (variety#)? 1

triple treat
```

Subroutine: Interpolation Search SS2TL2

PURPOSE:

Search a table of numeric keys.

The interpolation search mirrors the method most people use to find an item in a sorted list. If you were given the task of finding the key 777 in a list of, say, 20 records with sorted keys 1 to 1000, you would most likely start your search about three fourths of the way through the 20 records. You would use the key's value as an indicator of approximate position.

This subroutine uses the list of keys and the size of the list, and returns the position of the key in the list if it is found. Otherwise it returns a zero. In terms of speed, this search is about as fast as the binary search discussed in the first volume of Subroutine Sandwich.

REFERENCE:

M. van der Nat, "On Interpolation Search," *Communications of the ACM,* Vol. 22, No. 12, December 1979, p. 681.

LISTING:

```
1000 ' **** interpolation search
1010 L8=0 : R8=N+1
1020 X(L8)=X(1)-1 : X(R8)=X(N)+1
1030 X8=X(1) : X9=X(N) : S=0
1040 IF A<X8 OR A>X9 THEN RETURN
1050 IF R8<L8 THEN RETURN
1060 T8=L8+INT((R8-L8)*(A-X8)/(X9-X8)) : H8=X(T8)
1070 IF H8<>A
       THEN IF H8>=A
               THEN R8=T8-1 : X9=H8 : GOTO 1050
               ELSE L8=T8+1 : X8=H8 : GOTO 1050
       ELSE S=T8

1080 IF A<>X(S) THEN S=0
1090 RETURN
```

VARIABLES:

```
entering

    X:   List of numeric keys
    N:   Number of keys in X
    A:   Search argument

exiting

    S:   Position (subscript) of A in X

local

    L8:  Lower bound of interpolation search
    R8:  Upper bound of search
    X8:  Key at lower bound
    X9:  Key at upper bound
    T8:  Interpolated position in X for new comparison
    H8:  Key at interpolated position
```

NOTES:

All interpolation calculations are performed in line 1060. All other lines in the subroutine adjust the pointers to the list in one way or another.

The interpolation search is faster than the binary search in certain circumstances, specifically when the distribution of the keys is highly skewed. See the referenced article for a discussion of this procedure's place among the various searching techniques.

PROGRAM LISTING:

```
10 ' program : interpolation search : SS2TL2
20 ' authors : JOHN P GRILLO & JD ROBERTSON
30 '
40 CLEAR 1000
50 DIM X(10),X$(10)
60 PRINT
70 RESTORE
80 READ N
90 PRINT "element# - variety# / name;"
100 FOR I=1 TO N
110    READ X(I),X$(I)
120 NEXT I
130 W=2
140 GOSUB 2000    ' <<<< call columnar print routine
150 PRINT : PRINT
160 INPUT "input search argument (variety#)";A
170 IF A<0 THEN STOP
180 GOSUB 1000    ' <<<< call interpolation search
190 PRINT
200 IF S=0
      THEN PRINT "interpolation search unsuccessful"
      ELSE PRINT X$(S)
210 GOTO 60
220 DATA 8 :    ' watermelons
230 DATA 1,"sugar baby",4,"crimson sweet",5,"yellow baby"
240 DATA 8,"sweet favorite",11,"dixie queen",15,"top yield"
250 DATA 17,"charleston gray",18,"new hampshire midget"
260 STOP
1000 ' **** interpolation search
1010 L8=0 : R8=N+1
1020 X(L8)=X(1)-1 : X(R8)=X(N)+1
1030 X8=X(1) : X9=X(N) : S=0
1040 IF A<X8 OR A>X9 THEN RETURN
1050 IF R8<L8 THEN RETURN
1060 T8=L8+INT((R8-L8)*(A-X8)/(X9-X8)) : H8=X(T8)
1070 IF H8<>A
       THEN IF H8>=A
              THEN R8=T8-1 : X9=H8 : GOTO 1050
              ELSE L8=T8+1 : X8=H8 : GOTO 1050
       ELSE S=T8

1080 IF A<>X(S) THEN S=0
1090 RETURN
2000 ' #### columnar print routine
2010 P8$="## - ## / %                 %"
2020 L8=INT((N-1)/W) : M8=L8+1 : N8=N-W*L8
2030 IF N=INT(N/W)*W
       THEN L8=L8+1 : S8=1
       ELSE S8=0
```

```
2040 FOR I8=1 TO L8
2050     K8=0
2060     FOR J8=1 TO W
2070         PRINT USING P8$;I8+K8;X(I8+K8);X$(I8+K8);
2080         IF J8>N8 THEN K8=K8+L8 ELSE K8=K8+M8
2090     NEXT J8
2100 PRINT
2110 NEXT I8
2120 IF S8=1 THEN RETURN
2130 K8=0
2140 FOR J8=1 TO N8
2150     PRINT USING P8$;M8+K8;X(M8+K8);X$(M8+K8);
2160     K8=K8+M8
2170 NEXT J8
2180 PRINT
2190 RETURN
9999 END
```

RUN:

```
element# - variety# / name;
 1 -  1 / sugar baby          5 - 11 / dixie queen
 2 -  4 / crimson sweet       6 - 15 / top yield
 3 -  5 / yellow baby         7 - 17 / charleston gray
 4 -  8 / sweet favorite      8 - 18 / new hampshire mid

input search argument (variety#)? 11

dixie queen

element# - variety# / name;
 1 -  1 / sugar baby          5 - 11 / dixie queen
 2 -  4 / crimson sweet       6 - 15 / top yield
 3 -  5 / yellow baby         7 - 17 / charleston gray
 4 -  8 / sweet favorite      8 - 18 / new hampshire mid

input search argument (variety#)? 18

new hampshire midget

element# - variety# / name;
 1 -  1 / sugar baby          5 - 11 / dixie queen
 2 -  4 / crimson sweet       6 - 15 / top yield
 3 -  5 / yellow baby         7 - 17 / charleston gray
 4 -  8 / sweet favorite      8 - 18 / new hampshire mid

input search argument (variety#)? 13

interpolation search unsuccessful
```

Subroutine: Shuffle SS2UT1

PURPOSE:

Shuffle the pointers to a list.

"Shuffling" is a term familiar to those who play cards. In a computer program, a shuffle is useful when a list needs to be rearranged in random order again and again, for example, when testing various sorting techniques. Another application for shuffling a list in a program is to produce a randomly ordered set of pointers to another list. This latter indirect pointer shuffle is useful when programming simulations using Monte Carlo techniques.

This program shuffles the integers from 1 to N, which in turn serve as subscripts to a list of strings. A most valuable property of this shuffling technique is that the original list remains intact. In this case the list of strings is not disturbed. Only pointers to the list are shuffled.

REFERENCE:

Anthony Ralston, *Encyclopedia of Computer Science* (New York: Van Nostrand Reinhold, 1976), p. 943.

LISTING:

```
1000 ' **** shuffle
1010 RANDOM
1020 FOR I8=1 TO N
1030     R8=RND(N)
1040     T8=X(I8)
1050     X(I8)=X(R8)
1060     X(R8)=T8
1070 NEXT I8
1080 RETURN
```

VARIABLES:

```
entering

    X:   List of pointers to X$. Only these will
         be disturbed
    N:   Number of pointers in X

exiting

    X:   List of shuffled pointers

local

    I8:  Loop index
    R8:  Random pointer
    T8:  Temporary location for switch
```

NOTES:

The subroutine does a simple pick-and-switch between two randomly selected pointers to the list. The number of these pick-and-switch operations is N in this case. You should increase that number to a value larger than N if you want to maximize the shift of elements out of their original position.

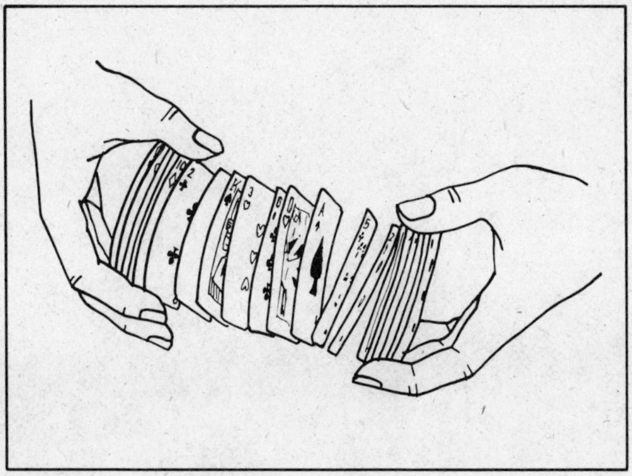

PROGRAM LISTING:

```
10 ' program : shuffle : SS2UT1
20 ' authors : JOHN P GRILLO & JD ROBERTSON
30 '
40 DIM X$(10),X(10)
50 PRINT
60 RESTORE
70 PRINT "original order"
80 READ N
90 FOR I=1 TO N
100   READ X$(I)
110   X(I)=I
120   IF I-INT(I/3)*3=1 THEN PRINT
130   PRINT USING "#### %                %";I,X$(I);
140 NEXT I
150 PRINT : PRINT : PRINT
160 GOSUB 1000    ' <<<< call shuffle
170 PRINT
180 PRINT "shuffled order"
190 FOR I=1 TO N
200    J=X(I)
210    IF I-INT(I/3)*3=1 THEN PRINT
220    PRINT USING "#### %                %";I;X$(J);
230 NEXT I
240 PRINT : PRINT
250 PRINT "continue ..."
260 FOR I=1 TO 200
270 IF INSTR(" ",INKEY$)=0 THEN 50
280 NEXT I
290 STOP
300 DATA 8 :   ' cucumbers
310 DATA "armenian","marketer","marketmore","poinsett"
320 DATA "straight eight","lemon","sunnybrook","spacemaster"
1000 ' **** shuffle
1010 RANDOM
1020 FOR I8=1 TO N
1030    R8=RND(N)
1040    T8=X(I8)
1050    X(I8)=X(R8)
1060    X(R8)=T8
1070 NEXT I8
1080 RETURN
9999 END
```

RUN:

```
original order

   1 armenian           2 marketer           3 marketmore
   4 poinsett           5 straight eight     6 lemon
   7 sunnybrook         8 spacemaster


shuffled order

   1 straight eight     2 lemon              3 marketer
   4 spacemaster        5 armenian           6 marketmore
   7 sunnybrook         8 poinsett

continue ...

original order

   1 armenian           2 marketer           3 marketmore
   4 poinsett           5 straight eight     6 lemon
   7 sunnybrook         8 spacemaster


shuffled order

   1 straight eight     2 poinsett           3 marketer
   4 lemon              5 spacemaster        6 sunnybrook
   7 marketmore         8 armenian

continue ...

original order

   1 armenian           2 marketer           3 marketmore
   4 poinsett           5 straight eight     6 lemon
   7 sunnybrook         8 spacemaster


shuffled order

   1 marketmore         2 poinsett           3 marketer
   4 lemon              5 spacemaster        6 armenian
   7 sunnybrook         8 straight eight

continue ...
```

MELVIN GARDENS
Deed
ST JEAN'S PLACE
DEED
SIDEWA
DEED
SUBTERRANEAN AVENUE
Deed

CHAPTER

10

BUSINESS

Introduction

The last chapter in this section of the book includes four subroutines that are commonly found in business applications. Any accounting information system uses at least one of these procedures for the calculation of depreciation. You may argue that one of these subroutines would have been enough, so why burden the book with four variations on the same theme? The reason is of course that different applications require different depreciation schedules. In times of high inflation, the double declining balance depreciation subroutine is particularly appropriate. But when the money supply is low, some other scheme could be used to more advantage. Certainly the user of any one of these routines should compare the output of all of them and then decide on the one to use.

Subroutine: Straight-Line Depreciation SS2BU1

PURPOSE:

Calculate straight-line depreciation.

Of all of the procedures for calculating depreciation, this one is the most common. The user supplies three values: initial cost, scrap value, and life of the asset in years. The subroutine produces a list of each year's depreciation.

This method for calculating depreciation is not to your advantage in times of high inflation, because the first year's depreciation is equal to the last. A better scheme would be to "load" the depreciation earlier in the asset's lifetime, which in effect would give you a better tax break when money is worth more.

REFERENCE:

Byron Gottfried, *Programming with BASIC*, Schaum's Outline Series (New York: McGraw-Hill, 1975), p. 58.

LISTING:

```
1000 ' **** straight-line depreciation
1010 D8=(C-S)/L
1020 FOR I8=1 TO L
1030    D(I8)=D8
1040 NEXT I8
1050 RETURN
```

VARIABLES:

```
entering

    C:   Cost of asset
    S:   Scrap value of asset
    L:   Life of asset

exiting

    D:   List of annual depreciation amounts

local

    D8:  Annual depreciation
    I8:  Loop index
```

NOTES:

The list D, which contains each year's depreciation, must be supplied by the calling program. If the programmer were to DIMension the list in the subroutine, that subroutine could be called only once, else an error would result from trying to redimension an array. You may wish to write this routine as a user-defined function, returning the amount (Cost–Scrap)/Life, since that is what happens here. We have elected to return a list D to conform more closely to the other depreciation algorithms, which follow.

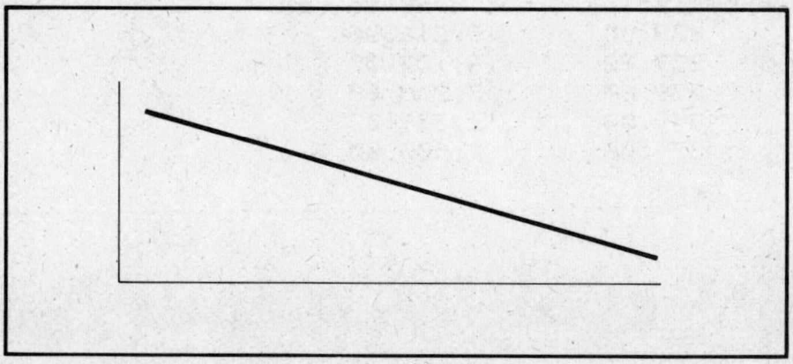

PROGRAM LISTING:

```
10 ' program : straight-line depreciation : SS2BU1
20 ' authors : JOHN P GRILLO & JD ROBERTSON
30 '
40 DIM D(20)
50 PRINT
60 PRINT "input cost, scrap value, & life of asset"
70 PRINT "  eg: 1000.00,100.00,7"
80 INPUT C,S,L
90 IF C<=0 THEN STOP
100 GOSUB 1000   ' <<<< call straight-line depreciation
110 PRINT
120 PRINT "straight-line depreciation
130 PRINT
140 B=C
150 PRINT "period";"   ";"depreciation";"    ";"net book value"
160 P$="####        ###,###.##      ###,###.##"
170 FOR I=1 TO L
180    B=B-D(I)
190    PRINT USING P$;I,D(I),B
200 NEXT I
210 GOTO 50
1000 ' **** straight-line depreciation
1010 D8=(C-S)/L
1020 FOR I8=1 TO L
1030    D(I8)=D8
1040 NEXT I8
1050 RETURN
9999 END
```

RUN:

```
input cost, scrap value, & life of asset
  eg: 1000.00,100.00,7
? 5895,1500,5

straight-line depreciation

period   depreciation   net book value
   1          879.00        5,016.00
   2          879.00        4,137.00
   3          879.00        3,258.00
   4          879.00        2,379.00
   5          879.00        1,500.00
```

RUN (CONTINUED):

```
input cost, scrap value, & life of asset
  eg: 1000.00,100.00,7
? 1000,100,7

straight-line depreciation

period   depreciation   net book value
   1          128.57          871.43
   2          128.57          742.86
   3          128.57          614.29
   4          128.57          485.71
   5          128.57          357.14
   6          128.57          228.57
   7          128.57          100.00

input cost, scrap value, & life of asset
  eg: 1000.00,100.00,7
? 100000,15000,20

straight-line depreciation

period   depreciation   net book value
   1        4,250.00       95,750.00
   2        4,250.00       91,500.00
   3        4,250.00       87,250.00
   4        4,250.00       83,000.00
   5        4,250.00       78,750.00
   6        4,250.00       74,500.00
   7        4,250.00       70,250.00
   8        4,250.00       66,000.00
   9        4,250.00       61,750.00
  10        4,250.00       57,500.00
  11        4,250.00       53,250.00
  12        4,250.00       49,000.00
  13        4,250.00       44,750.00
  14        4,250.00       40,500.00
  15        4,250.00       36,250.00
  16        4,250.00       32,000.00
  17        4,250.00       27,750.00
  18        4,250.00       23,500.00
  19        4,250.00       19,250.00
  20        4,250.00       15,000.00
```

Subroutine: Sum-of-Years' Digits Depreciation SS2BU2

PURPOSE:

Calculate depreciation using sum-of-years' digits.

This algorithm for calculating depreciation could be superior to the previous one, the straight-line formula. Here the total depreciable value (cost less scrap value) is subdivided into a series of amounts that are used as annual depreciation, but the annual amounts start high and end low. This allows higher depreciation earlier in the asset's life, thus reducing the effect of inflation.

It's called "sum-of-years' digits" because of the way it does its calculations. If the life of the asset is 4 years, say, the sum-of-years' digits is 4 + 3 + 2 + 1, or 10. The depreciable value is divided by 10 and the first year's depreciation is four-tenths; the second year, three-tenths; the third, two-tenths; and the last year, one-tenth.

REFERENCE:

Byron Gottfried, *Programming with BASIC*, Schaum's Outline Series (New York: McGraw-Hill, 1975), p. 58.

LISTING:

```
1000 ' **** sum-of-years' digits depreciation
1010 FOR I8=1 TO L
1020     D(I8)=2*(C-S)*(L+1-I8)/(L*(L+1))
1030 NEXT I8
1040 RETURN
```

VARIABLES:

```
entering

    C:   Cost of asset
    S:   Scrap value of asset
    L:   Lifetime of asset


exiting

    D:   List of annual depreciation amounts


local

    I8:  Loop index
```

NOTES:

In line 1020, the formula can be broken into two parts: First, the 2*(C–S) multiplier is constant for every iteration of the loop. Second, the fraction is the variable part. Notice that even the fraction's denominator remains constant throughout the loop's execution.

One good look at the output will demonstrate the procedure. The last year's depreciation is one "unit," the next-to-last year's depreciation is two of these units, and each prior year's depreciation is one more unit than the next.

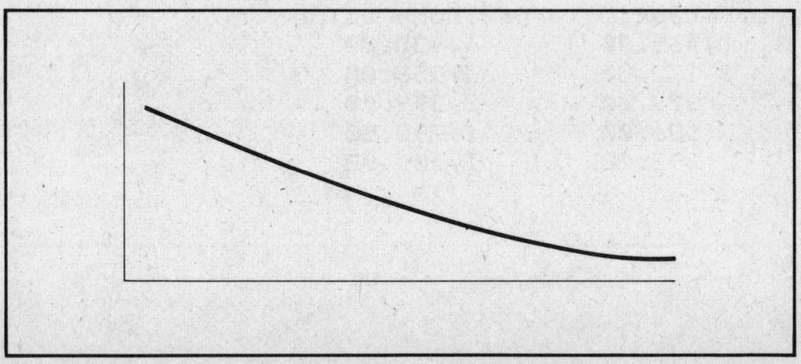

PROGRAM LISTING:

```
10 ' program : sum-of-years' digits depreciation : SS2BU2
20 ' authors : JOHN P GRILLO & JD ROBERTSON
30 '
40 DIM D(20)
50 PRINT
60 PRINT "input cost, scrap value, & life of asset"
70 PRINT "  eg: 1000.00,100.00,7"
80 INPUT C,S,L
90 IF C<=0 THEN STOP
100 GOSUB 1000   ' <<<< call sum-of-years' digits depreciation
110 PRINT
120 PRINT "sum-of-years' digits depreciation"
130 PRINT
140 B=C
150 PRINT "period";"   ";"depreciation";"   ";"net book value"
160 P$="####       ###,###.##      ###,###.##"
170 FOR I=1 TO L
180    B=B-D(I)
190    PRINT USING P$;I,D(I),B
200 NEXT I
210 GOTO 50
1000 ' **** sum-of-years' digits depreciation
1010 FOR I8=1 TO L
1020    D(I8)=2*(C-S)*(L+1-I8)/(L*(L+1))
1030 NEXT I8
1040 RETURN
9999 END
```

RUN:

```
input cost, scrap value, & life of asset
  eg: 1000.00,100.00,7
? 5895,1500,5

sum-of-years' digits depreciation

period   depreciation   net book value
   1         1,465.00        4,430.00
   2         1,172.00        3,258.00
   3           879.00        2,379.00
   4           586.00        1,793.00
   5           293.00        1,500.00
```

RUN (CONTINUED):

```
input cost, scrap value, & life of asset
  eg: 1000.00,100.00,7
? 1000,100,7

sum-of-years' digits depreciation

period   depreciation    net book value
   1          225.00          775.00
   2          192.86          582.14
   3          160.71          421.43
   4          128.57          292.86
   5           96.43          196.43
   6           64.29          132.14
   7           32.14          100.00

input cost, scrap value, & life of asset
  eg: 1000.00,100.00,7
? 100000,15000,20

sum-of-years' digits depreciation

period   depreciation    net book value
   1        8,095.24       91,904.80
   2        7,690.48       84,214.30
   3        7,285.71       76,928.60
   4        6,880.95       70,047.60
   5        6,476.19       63,571.40
   6        6,071.43       57,500.00
   7        5,666.67       51,833.30
   8        5,261.91       46,571.40
   9        4,857.14       41,714.30
  10        4,452.38       37,261.90
  11        4,047.62       33,214.30
  12        3,642.86       29,571.40
  13        3,238.10       26,333.30
  14        2,833.33       23,500.00
  15        2,428.57       21,071.40
  16        2,023.81       19,047.60
  17        1,619.05       17,428.60
  18        1,214.29       16,214.30
  19          809.52       15,404.80
  20          404.76       15,000.00
```

Subroutine: Declining-Balance Depreciation SS2BU3

PURPOSE:

Calculate declining-balance depreciation of an asset.

Even better than the sum-of-years' digits method for calculating depreciation during times of inflation is this algorithm. The asset depreciates most of the first year, and less and less every successive year.

As with the other depreciation subroutines supplied in this book, the calling program supplies the cost, scrap value, and life of the asset. The subroutine returns a list of the annual depreciation amounts.

REFERENCE:

Byron Gottfried, *Programming with BASIC,* Schaum's Outline Series (New York: McGraw-Hill, 1975), p. 58.

LISTING:

```
1000 ' **** declining balance depreciation
1010 A8=0
1020 FOR I8=1 TO L
1030    D(I8)=(1-(S/C)↑(1/L))*(C-A8)
1040   A8=A8+D(I8)
1050 NEXT I8
1060 RETURN
```

VARIABLES:

```
entering

    C:   Cost of asset
    S:   Scrap value of asset (must not be zero)
    L:   Life of asset

exiting

    D:   List of annual depreciation amounts

local

    A8:  Accumulated depreciation
    I8:  Loop index
```

NOTES:

The formula in line 1030 calculates the I8th year's depreciation based on the amounts S, C, and L, and also the amount A8, which represents the amount of depreciation taken so far. As A8 increases, the amount of depreciation D(I8) decreases.

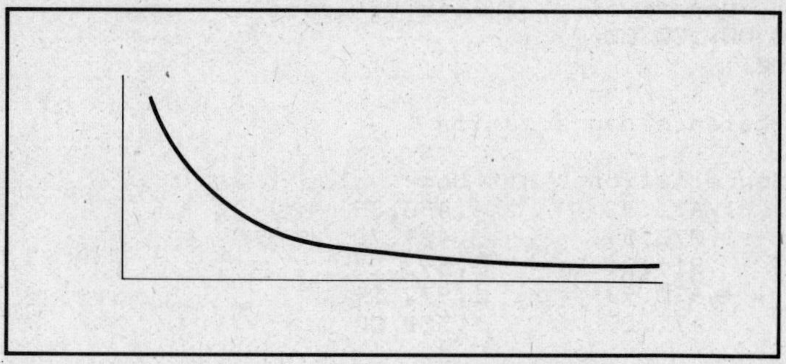

PROGRAM LISTING:

```
10 ' program : declining balance depreciation : SS2BU3
20 ' authors : JOHN P GRILLO & JD ROBERTSON
30 '
40 DIM D(20)
50 PRINT
60 PRINT "input cost, scrap value, & life of asset"
70 PRINT "  eg: 1000.00,100.00,7"
80 INPUT C,S,L
90 IF C<=0 THEN STOP
100 GOSUB 1000   ' <<<< call declining balance depreciation
110 PRINT
120 PRINT "declining balance depreciation"
130 PRINT
140 B=C
150 PRINT "period";"   ";"depreciation";"   ";"net book value"
160 P$="####        ###,###.##      ###,###.##"
170 FOR I=1 TO L
180    B=B-D(I)
190    PRINT USING P$;I,D(I),B
200 NEXT I
210 GOTO 50
1000 ' **** declining balance depreciation
1010 A8=0
1020 FOR I8=1 TO L
1030    D(I8)=(1-(S/C)↑(1/L))*(C-A8)
1040    A8=A8+D(I8)
1050 NEXT I8
1060 RETURN
9999 END
```

RUN:

```
input cost, scrap value, & life of asset
  eg: 1000.00,100.00,7
? 5895,1500,5

declining balance depreciation

period   depreciation   net book value
   1        1,411.62       4,483.38
   2        1,073.59       3,409.78
   3          816.51       2,593.27
   4          620.99       1,972.29
   5          472.29       1,500.00
```

RUN (CONTINUED):

```
input cost, scrap value, & life of asset
  eg: 1000.00,100.00,7
? 1000,100,7

declining balance depreciation

period    depreciation    net book value
   1          280.31          719.69
   2          201.74          517.95
   3          145.19          372.76
   4          104.49          268.27
   5           75.20          193.07
   6           54.12          138.95
   7           38.95          100.00

input cost, scrap value, & life of asset
  eg: 1000.00,100.00,7
? 100000,15000,20

declining balance depreciation

period    depreciation    net book value
   1        9,049.61       90,950.40
   2        8,230.66       82,719.70
   3        7,485.82       75,233.90
   4        6,808.38       68,425.60
   5        6,192.25       62,233.30
   6        5,631.87       56,601.40
   7        5,122.21       51,479.20
   8        4,658.67       46,820.60
   9        4,237.08       42,583.50
  10        3,853.64       38,729.80
  11        3,504.90       35,224.90
  12        3,187.72       32,037.20
  13        2,899.24       29,138.00
  14        2,636.87       26,501.10
  15        2,398.25       24,102.90
  16        2,181.21       21,921.60
  17        1,983.82       19,937.80
  18        1,804.29       18,133.50
  19        1,641.01       16,492.50
  20        1,492.51       15,000.00
```

Subroutine: Double-Declining-Balance Depreciation SS2BU4

PURPOSE:

Calculate the double-declining-balance depreciation of an asset.

The calling routine supplies cost, scrap value, and life of asset, as usual. The subroutine returns the list of annual depreciation amounts. All of this conforms to the previous subroutines. However, this one is the best of the lot during times of high inflation, because it depreciates the asset most during the first few years.

REFERENCE:

Byron Gottfried, *Programming with BASIC*, Schaum's Outline Series (New York: McGraw-Hill, 1975), p. 58. One of us (JDR) modified the cited method to convert to straight-line depreciation halfway through the asset's life.

LISTING:

```
1000 ' **** double declining balance depreciation
1010 A8=0 : R8=2/L
1020 I8=1 : K8=INT((L+1)/2)+1
1030 D(I8)=R8*(C-S-A8)
1040 A8=A8+D(I8)
1050 I8=I8+1
1060 IF I8>L THEN RETURN
1070 IF I8<K8
        THEN 1030
        ELSE IF I8>K8
                THEN D(I8)=D(I8-1)
                ELSE D(I8)=(C-S-A8)/(L+1-K8)
1080 GOTO 1040
```

VARIABLES:

```
entering

    C:    Cost of asset
    S:    Scrap value of asset
    L:    Life of asset

exiting

    D:    List of annual depreciation amounts

local

    A8:    Accumulated depreciation
    R8:    Multiplication factor
    I8:    Loop index
    K8:    Constant representing the asset's half-life
```

NOTES:

This procedure looks complex because it is made up of two algorithms. For the first half of the asset's life, the depreciation algorithm uses a form of the declining-balance procedure. Then it switches over to the straight-line depreciation formula. That is why the output shows equal amounts of depreciation during the last half of the item's lifetime. The reason for using this scheme is to depreciate the item as much as possible during the first half of its life, then to maintain a constant and relatively small amount of depreciation during the last half of the item's lifetime.

The subroutine is complex. The asset's value decreases by a constant percentage each year. Thus the actual amount of the depreciation varies year by year. A depreciation factor is calculated (2/life of the asset), and that factor is multiplied by the value of the asset at the beginning of each year.

PROGRAM LISTING:

```
10 ' program : double declining balance depreciation : SS2BU4
20 ' authors : JOHN P GRILLO & JD ROBERTSON
30 '
40 DIM D(20)
50 PRINT
60 PRINT "input cost, scrap value, & life of asset"
70 PRINT "  eg: 1000.00,100.00,7"
80 INPUT C,S,L
90 IF C<=0 THEN STOP
100 GOSUB 1000   ' <<<< call double declining balance deprec
110 PRINT
120 PRINT "double declining balance depreciation"
130 PRINT
140 B=C
150 PRINT "period";"   ";"depreciation";"   ";"net book value"
160 P$="####       ###,###.##      ###,###.##"
170 FOR I=1 TO L
180     B=B-D(I)
190     PRINT USING P$;I,D(I),B
200 NEXT I
210 GOTO 50
1000 ' **** double declining balance depreciation
1010 A8=0 : R8=2/L
1020 I8=1 : K8=INT((L+1)/2)+1
1030 D(I8)=R8*(C-S-A8)
1040 A8=A8+D(I8)
1050 I8=I8+1
1060 IF I8>L THEN RETURN
1070 IF I8<K8
        THEN 1030
        ELSE IF I8>K8
               THEN D(I8)=D(I8-1)
               ELSE D(I8)=(C-S-A8)/(L+1-K8)
1080 GOTO 1040
9999 END
```

RUN:

```
input cost, scrap value, & life of asset
  eg: 1000.00,100.00,7
? 5895,1500,5

double declining balance depreciation

period   depreciation   net book value
   1        1,758.00        4,137.00
   2        1,054.80        3,082.20
   3          632.88        2,449.32
   4          474.66        1,974.66
   5          474.66        1,500.00
```

RUN (CONTINUED):

```
input cost, scrap value, & life of asset
  eg: 1000.00,100.00,7
? 1000,100,7

double declining balance depreciation

period   depreciation    net book value
   1          257.14          742.86
   2          183.67          559.18
   3          131.20          427.99
   4           93.71          334.28
   5           78.09          256.18
   6           78.09          178.09
   7           78.09          100.00

input cost, scrap value, & life of asset
  eg: 1000.00,100.00,7
? 100000,15000,20

double declining balance depreciation

period   depreciation    net book value
   1        8,500.00       91,500.00
   2        7,650.00       83,850.00
   3        6,885.00       76,965.00
   4        6,196.50       70,768.50
   5        5,576.85       65,191.70
   6        5,019.17       60,172.50
   7        4,517.25       55,655.20
   8        4,065.52       51,589.70
   9        3,658.97       47,930.70
  10        3,293.07       44,637.70
  11        2,963.77       41,673.90
  12        2,963.77       38,710.10
  13        2,963.77       35,746.40
  14        2,963.77       32,782.60
  15        2,963.77       29,818.80
  16        2,963.77       26,855.10
  17        2,963.77       23,891.30
  18        2,963.77       20,927.50
  19        2,963.77       17,963.80
  20        2,963.77       15,000.00
```

PART III

Mother Programs

Introduction

The fine art of incorporating subroutines into larger programs rests primarily on the programmer's skill in being able to satisfy a user's need. Good programs are not simply developed, as is, from the blue. Rather, they are designed carefully to justify a long and useful life in the user's library. Initial attention to their design is essential so that they can be modified later as new modules are added and old ones are improved or replaced.

Designing good programs requires a disciplined approach. To accomplish this, we suggest the following outline for successful program design:

1. Understand the user's problem
2. Design the program's modular structure
3. Design the program's outputs
4. Design the program's inputs
5. Design the program's storage needs
6. Design the program's processes
   a. Pseudocode
   b. Code
   c. Test and run
7. Document

Of course we can't guarantee a program that runs the first time if you perform each of these steps in this order, but we can assure you that the likelihood of creating a program that runs the first time is greatly increased if you do so. We have taught programmers at all levels of expertise for a long time, and we find this approach to generating code to be the one that ensures the most success. We used it in coding the following mother programs, and we will demonstrate the technique using these programs as vehicles for the discussion.

CHAPTER

11

RESORT TIME-SHARING WEEKS

Introduction

The intent of this program is to provide a calendar for a highly specific application: the resort that sells vacation weeks starting on a Saturday afternoon and ending on a Saturday morning. The buyer stipulates which week he or she desires, and the resort sells a shared ownership of a condominium, cabin, resort hotel, or whatever.

The applications in which this program can serve as a model are numerous and varied. For example, a college registrar may want to set up a six-week summer session starting during the last full week of May. Or a firm may want to print a calendar of all holidays scheduled during a given year. Perhaps a committee wants to select meeting times. All such applications could be accommodated easily by this program.

Mother Program 1: Resort Time-sharing Weeks

User's Problem Statement

The program calculates and prints out a table of 52 weekly intervals. All that the user is required to supply is the year for which the weekly calendar is to be produced. Although we suggest that the program be used in determining the dates that bracket a given week at a resort, it could fulfill other applications. For example, a school could use it to establish its yearly academic calendar.

Structure Chart

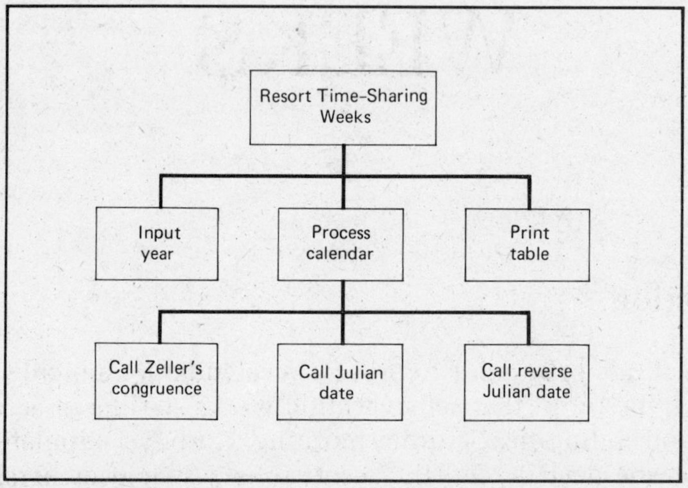

Output Design

The screen display shows a two-column table; the first is the 52 weeks of the year and the second is the two dates that bracket each week. Each column has headings.

Inputs

The computer asks, "enter year for which weeks are to be determined," and the user responds with the four-digit year, for example, 1990 or 1987.

Storage

This program is singular in that it doesn't use any arrays whatsoever. It produces each line of the table one at a time, calculating its answers as it goes. Note, however, that in line 160 it uses N# as a variable, which is a double precision variable. The necessity for this is explained in Chapter 3 of the text, in which the reverse Julian date algorithm is discussed.

Processing

PSEUDOCODE

```
1.  Get user's choice of year
2.  Find first Saturday after January 3 (call Zeller's
    congruence)
3.  Get unique 7-digit integer N# (call Julian date)
4.  Print heading for table
5.  For L=1 to 52 do:
        Print week number L
        Print date of first day of week
        Add 7 to Julian date N#
        Get date of last day of this week
          (call reverse Julian date)
        Print date of last day of week
    Enddo
```

CODE

PROGRAM LISTING:

```
10 ' program : resort timesharing weeks : SS2MOTH1
20 ' authors : JD ROBERTSON & JOHN P GRILLO
30 '
40 INPUT "enter year for which weeks are to be determined";I
50 J=1
60 FOR K=4 TO 10
70    GOSUB 1000   ' <<<< call Zeller's congruence
80    IF N=6 THEN 100
90 NEXT K
100 GOSUB 2000   ' <<<< call Julian date
110 PRINT "week";TAB(17);"resort year";I
120 PRINT "----";TAB(17);"----------------"
130 FOR L=1 TO 52
140    IF (L=14) OR (L=40) THEN PRINT L;"*", ELSE PRINT L,
150    PRINT USING "## / ##";J,K;
160    N#=N#+7
170    GOSUB 3000   ' <<<< call reverse Julian date
180    PRINT USING " - ## / ##";J;K
190 NEXT L
200 STOP
1000 ' **** Zeller's congruence
1010 IF J>2
       THEN M8=J-2  : Y8=I
       ELSE M8=J+10 : Y8=I-1
1020 C8=INT(Y8/100) : D8=Y8-100*C8
1030 N=INT((13*M8-1)/5)+K+D8+INT(D8/4)+INT(C8/4)-C8-C8+77
1040 N=N-7*INT(N/7)
1050 RETURN
2000 ' **** Julian date
2010  IF J>2
        THEN M8=J-3 : Y8=I
        ELSE M8=J+9 : Y8=I-1
2020  C8=INT(Y8/100) : D8=Y8-100*C8
2030  N#=INT(146097*C8/4)+K+INT(1461*D8/4)+1721119
          +INT((153*M8+2)/5)
2040 RETURN
```

PROGRAM LISTING (CONTINUED):

```
3000 ' **** reverse Julian date
3010 M8=N#-1721119 : I=INT((4*M8-1)/146097)
3020 M8=4*M8-1-146097*I : K=INT(M8/4)
3030 M8=INT((4*K+3)/1461) : K=4*K+3-1461*M8
3040 K=INT((K+4)/4) : J=INT((5*K-3)/153)
3050 K=5*K-3-153*J : K=INT((K+5)/5)
3060 I=100*I+M8
3070 IF J<10
       THEN J=J+3
       ELSE J=J-9 : I=I+1
3080 RETURN
9999 END
```

TEST AND RUN:

PROGRAM OUTPUT:

```
enter year for which weeks are to be determined? 1983
week              resort year 1983
----              ----------------
 1                1 /  8 -  1 / 15
 2                1 / 15 -  1 / 22
 3                1 / 22 -  1 / 29
 4                1 / 29 -  2 /  5
 5                2 /  5 -  2 / 12
 6                2 / 12 -  2 / 19
 7                2 / 19 -  2 / 26
 8                2 / 26 -  3 /  5
 9                3 /  5 -  3 / 12
 10               3 / 12 -  3 / 19
```

PROGRAM OUTPUT (CONTINUED):

```
11                 3 / 19 -  3 / 26
12                 3 / 26 -  4 /  2
13                 4 /  2 -  4 /  9
14  *              4 /  9 -  4 / 16
15                 4 / 16 -  4 / 23
16                 4 / 23 -  4 / 30
17                 4 / 30 -  5 /  7
18                 5 /  7 -  5 / 14
19                 5 / 14 -  5 / 21
20                 5 / 21 -  5 / 28
21                 5 / 28 -  6 /  4
22                 6 /  4 -  6 / 11
23                 6 / 11 -  6 / 18
24                 6 / 18 -  6 / 25
25                 6 / 25 -  7 /  2
26                 7 /  2 -  7 /  9
27                 7 /  9 -  7 / 16
28                 7 / 16 -  7 / 23
29                 7 / 23 -  7 / 30
30                 7 / 30 -  8 /  6
31                 8 /  6 -  8 / 13
32                 8 / 13 -  8 / 20
33                 8 / 20 -  8 / 27
34                 8 / 27 -  9 /  3
35                 9 /  3 -  9 / 10
36                 9 / 10 -  9 / 17
37                 9 / 17 -  9 / 24
38                 9 / 24 - 10 /  1
39                10 /  1 - 10 /  8
40  *             10 /  8 - 10 / 15
41                10 / 15 - 10 / 22
42                10 / 22 - 10 / 29
43                10 / 29 - 11 /  5
44                11 /  5 - 11 / 12
45                11 / 12 - 11 / 19
46                11 / 19 - 11 / 26
47                11 / 26 - 12 /  3
48                12 /  3 - 12 / 10
49                12 / 10 - 12 / 17
50                12 / 17 - 12 / 24
51                12 / 24 - 12 / 31
52                12 / 31 -  1 /  7
```

Documentation

NOTES:

Lines 60 through 90 search the calendar using Zeller's congruence to find the date of the first Saturday after the third of January. That date will establish the beginning of the first week of the resort calendar year.

Line 100 calls the Julian date subroutine to find the unique 7-digit number that corresponds to that Saturday.

Lines 110 and 120 print the column headings.

Lines 130 through 190 comprise the body of the program, which is the 52-week loop. The reason for line 140 printing an asterisk on those two selected 14th and 40th weeks is to indicate that those weeks are used for scheduled maintenance of the resort.

The annotation of these two weeks for maintenance could become an easy and useful embellishment to the program. The resort owner could provide annotated calendars for each client. In these customized runs, the program asks the user for two selected weeks, say A and B. Line 140 is rewritten as:

```
140 IF (L=A) OR (L=B) THEN PRINT L;"*", ELSE PRINT L,
```

This way the program flags those two weeks for the resort's clients.

CHAPTER

12

TEXT IN ADJACENT COLUMNS

Introduction

This type of program is most commonly found in the computer systems that newspapers and magazines use to set their print. More and more of these publishers are using computers and their associated word processing programs to set their type. The program we have included here prints a set of columns down a page. The user enters the number of columns and the width of each column. The computer in return prints the text in those columns side by side, each column approximately the same length.

Mother Program 2: Text in Adjacent Columns

User's Problem Statement

The program prepares string text to be printed in one or more columns across the printed page or the screen. The data strings that the program processes are in this case stored within DATA statements in the program. The specific requirements of this program include the number of columns and the width of each of the columns.

Structure Chart:

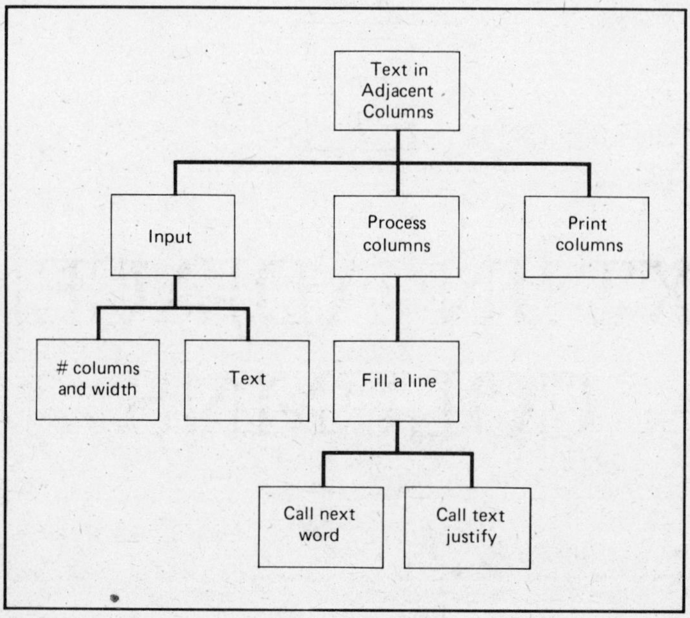

Output Design

The screen displays the columns of text next to each other. Each column is right-justified within its defined length as determined by the user. Two spaces separate the columns vertically.

Inputs

The user supplies the number of columns and the width of each column. The data is in DATA statements and the rules for column design are defined within the program.

Storage

The program copies all DATA strings into an array T$. During processing a second array X$ is filled with the processed output lines, each one being one column wide. Depending on the length of the text being processed, whether it is in DATA statements as in this program or on a sequential file, the program must accommodate an appropriate number of output lines in its DIM statement.

Processing

PSEUDOCODE

```
1. Copy DATA strings to T$ array
2. Define width and column number parameters
3. For J=1 to end of T$ array do:
      Fill a line
         (call buffer fill),
         (call next word)
      Justify the line
         (call text justify)
      Store prepared line in X$( J)
   Enddo
4. Print two-column output
      (call columnar print)
```

CODE

PROGRAM LISTING:

```
10 ' program : text in adjacent columns : SS2MOTH2
20 ' authors : JOHN P GRILLO & JD ROBERTSON
30 '
40 CLEAR 10000
50 DIM T$(50),X$(180)
60 READ N
70 FOR I=1 TO N
80    READ T$(I)
90 NEXT I
100 T$(N)=T$(N)+" #"
110 G=0 : K=1 : T=1
120 INPUT "input buffer width";W
130 INPUT "input number of columns";A
140 J=0
150 GOSUB 2000    ' <<<< call buffer fill
160 IF G=1 THEN L=1
170 J=J+1
180 GOSUB 3000    ' <<<< call text justify
190 PRINT J,B$
200 X$(J)=B$
210 IF G<>1 THEN 150
220 CLS
230 GOSUB 4000    ' <<<< call columnar print routine
240 STOP
250 DATA 31 :    ' okra, radishes, & peanuts
260 DATA "Okra can be grown in a sunny area where days and"
270 DATA "nights are warm.  Pods add body and flavor when"
280 DATA "cut up in soups, stews, catsup, and relishes."
290 DATA "Also delicious as a cooked vegetable.  Pick"
300 DATA "every two or three days for a continuous harvest."
310 DATA "Pods are best when young and small.  A packet of"
320 DATA "seeds will sow 15 ft. of row; one oz., 50 ft."
330 DATA "Radishes thrive and develop best flavor in cool"
340 DATA "weather when growth is quick and steady.  Sow seeds"
350 DATA "in spring as early as the soil can be deeply worked;"
360 DATA "repeat planting at 10-day intervals until early"
370 DATA "summer, then again a month before frost.  A packet"
380 DATA "contains approximately 400 seeds, and will sow about"
390 DATA "20 feet. of row; one oz., 100 ft.  When sowing"
400 DATA "beets, carrots, parsley, and parsnips, mix in a few"
410 DATA "radish seeds to mark rows for these slower growing"
420 DATA "vegetables."
```

PROGRAM LISTING (CONTINUED):

```
430 DATA "Peanuts, traditionally a Southern crop, grow well"
440 DATA "anywhere with hot summers and 4-5 frost-free months."
450 DATA "Kids love these fascinating plants, whose long"
460 DATA "slender shoots dig into the ground to form the"
470 DATA "peanuts.  After all danger of frost, plant seeds"
480 DATA "---in or out of shells--- 4 to 6 in. apart, 2 in."
490 DATA "deep, in rows 3 ft. apart.  Before frost, dig up the"
500 DATA "entire plant and air-dry to cure before removing"
510 DATA "pods.  Under favorable conditions in the South, each"
520 DATA "plant yields about 50-60 pods; elsewhere, about"
530 DATA "30-40 pods.  Roast peanuts at 350 degrees F. for"
540 DATA "about 20 minutes.  Peanuts are one of the best"
550 DATA "garden sources for protein and make healthful"
560 DATA "snacks."
1000 ' **** next word
1010 W$=""
1020 IF G=1 THEN RETURN
1030 FOR I8=T TO LEN(T$(K))
1040     M8$=MID$(T$(K),I8,1)
1050     IF M8$="#" THEN G=1 : RETURN
1060     IF M8$<>" " THEN 1100
1070 NEXT I8
1080 K=K+1 : T=1
1090 IF W$=""
       THEN 1030
       ELSE G=0 : RETURN
1100 W$=W$+M8$
1110 IF I8=LEN(T$(K))
       THEN K=K+1 : T=1 :
            G=0 : RETURN
1120 FOR J8=I8+1 TO LEN(T$(K))
1130     M8$=MID$(T$(K),J8,1)
1140     IF M8$=" " THEN T=J8 : GOTO 1180
1150     W$=W$+M8$
1160 NEXT J8
1170 K=K+1 : T=1
1180 G=0
1190 RETURN
2000 ' **** buffer fill
2010 B$=""
2020 IF W$=""
       THEN GOSUB 1000    ' <<<< call next word
2030 IF G=1 THEN RETURN
2040 IF LEN(B$)+LEN(W$)<=W-1
       THEN B$=B$+W$+" " : W$="" : GOTO 2020
2050 IF RIGHT$(B$,1)=" " THEN B$=LEFT$(B$,LEN(B$)-1)
2060 RETURN
```

PROGRAM LISTING (CONTINUED):

```
3000 ' **** text justify
3010 RANDOM
3020 N8=W-LEN(B$)
3030 IF N8=0 THEN RETURN
3040 IF L=1 THEN B$=B$+STRING$(W-LEN(B$)," ") : RETURN
3050 IF INSTR(B$," ")=0 THEN B$=B$+" "
3060 J8=1
3070 FOR I8=1 TO N8
3080    J8=INSTR(J8,B$," ")
3090    IF J8=0 THEN J8=RND(LEN(B$)) : GOTO 3080
3100    IF RND(2)>1
          THEN B$=LEFT$(B$,J8)+" "+RIGHT$(B$,LEN(B$)-J8)
          ELSE J8=J8+1 : GOTO 3080
3110    J8=J8+2
3120 NEXT I8
3130 RETURN
4000 ' **** columnar print routine
4010 P8$="%"+STRING$(W+1," ")+"%"
4020 L8=INT((J-1)/A) : M8=L8+1 : N8=J-A*L8
4030 IF J=INT(J/A)*A
       THEN L8=L8+1 : S8=1
       ELSE S8=0
4040 FOR I8=1 TO L8
4050    K8=0
4060    FOR J8=1 TO A
4070       PRINT USING P8$;X$(I8+K8);
4080       IF J8>N8 THEN K8=K8+L8 ELSE K8=K8+M8
4090    NEXT J8
4100 PRINT
4110 NEXT I8
4120 IF S8=1 THEN RETURN
4130 K8=0
4140 FOR J8=1 TO N8
4150    PRINT USING P8$;X$(M8+K8);
4160    K8=K8+M8
4170 NEXT J8
4180 PRINT
4190 RETURN
9999 END
```

TEST AND RUN

PROGRAM OUTPUT:

```
input buffer width? 28
input number of columns? 2
 1              Okra   can   be  grown  in a
 2              sunny  area where  days  and
 3              nights  are warm.  Pods  add
 4              body and flavor  when cut up
 5              in   soups,  stews,  catsup,
 6              and  relishes.          Also
 7              delicious  as    a    cooked
 8              vegetable.  Pick   every two
 9              or three   days   for      a
 10             continuous  harvest.    Pods
 11             are best when  young     and
 12             small.  A  packet   of seeds
 13             will  sow 15 ft. of row; one
 14             oz., 50 ft.  Radishes thrive
 15             and  develop  best flavor in
 16             cool  weather when growth is
 17             quick  and steady. Sow seeds
 18             in  spring  as early  as the
 19             soil can  be  deeply worked;
 20             repeat planting  at  10-day
 21             intervals    until     early
 22             summer, then  again  a month
 23             before  frost.    A   packet
 24             contains  approximately  400
 25             seeds,  and  will sow  about
 26             20  feet. of  row;  one oz.,
 27             100  ft.  When sowing beets,
 28             carrots,    parsley,     and
 29             parsnips,  mix   in a   few
 30             radish  seeds  to mark  rows
 31             for these   slower   growing
 32             vegetables.         Peanuts,
 33             traditionally  a   Southern
 34             crop, grow   well   anywhere
 35             with hot  summers  and   4-5
 36             frost-free     months.  Kids
 37             love  these      fascinating
 38             plants, whose  long  slender
 39             shoots  dig  into the ground
 40             to  form the peanuts.  After
 41             all danger of  frost,  plant
 42             seeds  ---in   or   out   of
 43             shells--- 4 to  6 in. apart,
 44             2 in. deep, in   rows  3 ft.
```

PROGRAM OUTPUT (CONTINUED):

```
45          apart.  Before frost, dig up
46          the entire   plant        and
47          air-dry  to  cure     before
48          removing    pods.      Under
49          favorable  conditions in the
50          South, each   plant   yields
51          about       50-60       pods;
52          elsewhere,     about    30-40
53          pods. Roast  peanuts at  350
54          degrees  F.   for  about  20
55          minutes. Peanuts  are one of
56          the best  garden sources for
57          protein and  make  healthful
58          snacks.
```

```
Okra   can   be  grown  in a
sunny  area where  days  and
nights  are warm.  Pods  add
body and flavor  when cut up
in   soups,  stews,  catsup,
and  relishes.          Also
delicious   as    a   cooked
vegetable.  Pick   every two
or three   days   for      a
continuous  harvest.    Pods
are best when  young     and
small.  A  packet   of seeds
will  sow 15 ft. of row; one
oz., 50 ft.  Radishes thrive
and  develop  best flavor in
cool  weather when growth is
quick  and steady. Sow seeds
in  spring  as early  as the
soil can  be  deeply worked;
repeat planting  at   10-day
intervals   until      early
summer, then  again  a month
before  frost.    A   packet
contains  approximately  400
seeds,  and  will sow  about
20  feet. of  row;  one oz.,
100  ft.  When sowing beets,
carrots,    parsley,     and
parsnips,  mix    in a   few
radish  seeds  to mark  rows
for these   slower   growing
vegetables.         Peanuts,
traditionally   a   Southern
crop, grow    well  anywhere
with hot  summers  and   4-5
frost-free    months.   Kids
love  these      fascinating
plants, whose  long  slender
shoots  dig  into the ground
to  form the peanuts.  After
all danger of  frost,  plant
seeds  ---in    or   out  of
shells--- 4 to  6 in. apart,
2 in. deep, in   rows  3 ft.
apart.  Before frost, dig up
the entire   plant       and
air-dry  to  cure     before
removing    pods.      Under
favorable  conditions in the
South, each   plant   yields
about       50-60      pods;
elsewhere,     about   30-40
pods. Roast  peanuts at  350
degrees  F.   for  about  20
minutes. Peanuts  are one of
the best  garden sources for
protein and  make  healthful
snacks.
```

Documentation

NOTES:

Line 40 clears 10000 characters of memory for string workspace. This may seem like a lot, but remember that this program keeps the data in three different places during its execution: DATA statements, the T$ array, and the X$ array.

Line 60 defines N as the number of DATA statements that contain strings to be processed.

Lines 70–90 fill the T$ array.

Lines 100–130 set up the parameters, such as the number of columns and the width of each column. Line 100 supplies the pair of terminator symbols "_#" required by the next word subroutine.

Lines 150–210 comprise the loop of the program. Each iteration of the loop produces one right-justified line and stores in X$.

Line 230 calls a subroutine that prints the results.

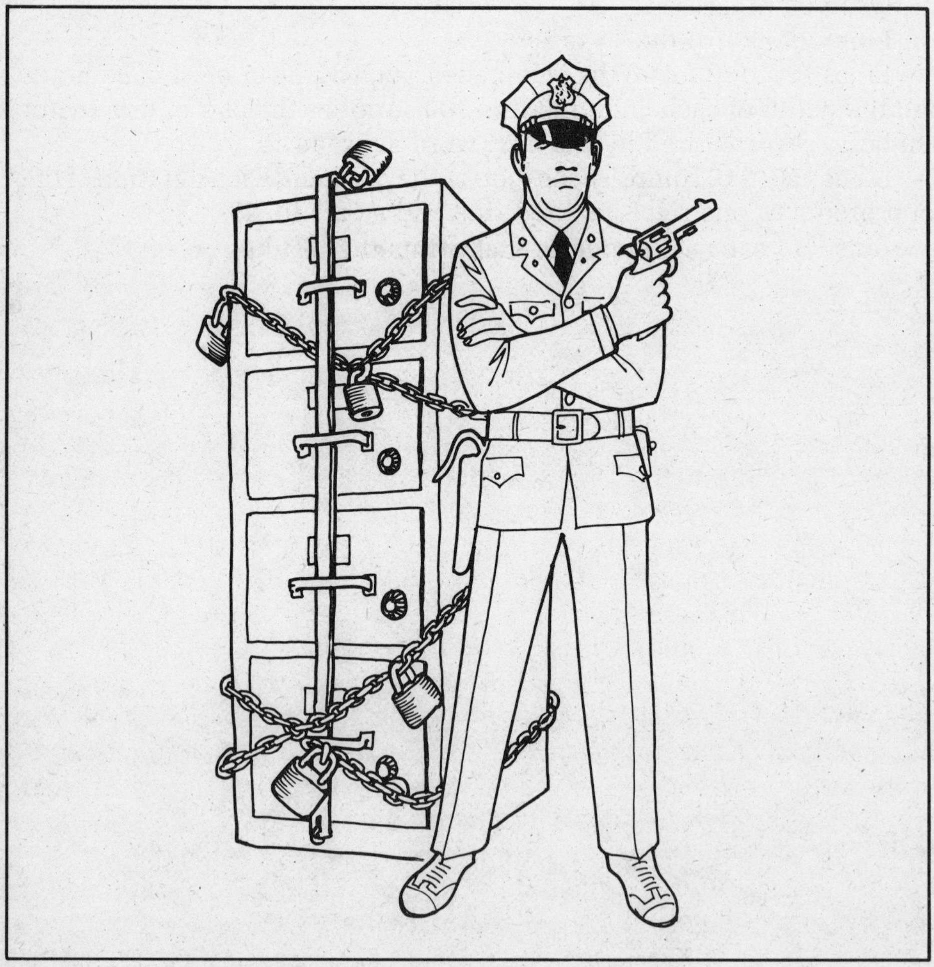

CHAPTER

13

FILE PROTECTION

Introduction

The proliferation of microcomputers has made the individuals who own them acutely aware that the programs and data on the diskettes are pretty much up for grabs. They are easy to copy, and therefore they are easy to steal and to distribute to anyone with the same type of hardware. Many software producers have worked hard to protect their investment of time and effort by rewriting their applications in assembly language, or by having their programs compiled into machine language by a BASIC compiler. Both of these schemes leave a lot to be desired, since they both involve a considerable expense of time and money.

The program we include in this chapter could be used with minor expansion to take a BASIC program or a data file and to encode it into a rather incomprehensible gibberish unless the password is known. We encourage you to experiment with it and to determine on your own which process of encryption you prefer.

Mother Program 3: File Protection

User's Problem Statement

The purpose of this program is to protect files of text data. The user has a choice of several activities, including the creation or display of a text file, or its encoding or decoding. The usual sequence of activities would be for the user to create a text file, encode it, store it in encoded mode, and later to decode and display the file.

Structure Chart

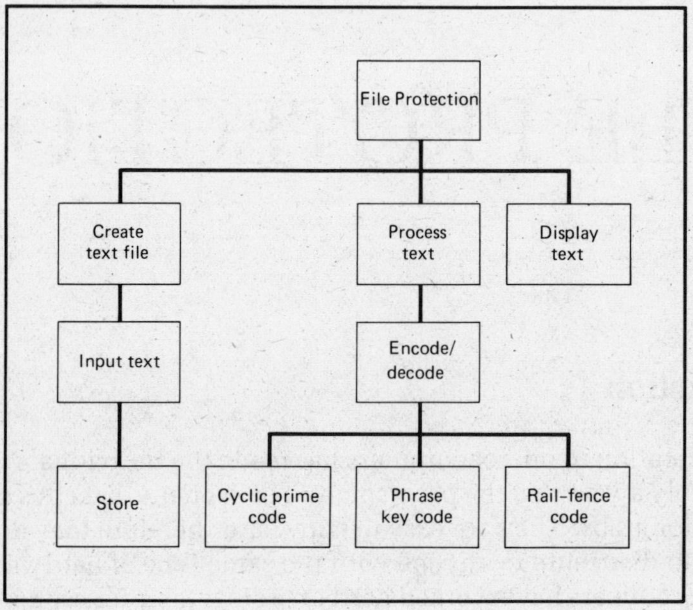

Output Design

The first portion of output that needs careful design is the menu display from which the user selects the activity to be performed. The menu should have these activities, at least as a start:

1. Create text file
2. Encode text file using cyclic prime code
3. phrase key code
4. rail-fence code
5. Decode text file using cyclic prime code
6. phrase key code
7. rail-fence code
8. View text tile
9. Stop

Aside from the menu and the dialog produced during the encode-decode processing of the text, the only output is produced when the user requests activity 8 to view the text file. The display includes both the lines of text and the record number being displayed. Thus the user can verify that all records are shown.

Inputs:

If the user selects activity 1 to create a text file, the dialog is (C* is computer, U* is user):

```
C*  enter name of text file to be created
U*  zugzug
C*  enter text line #1
U*  George Washington Carver, famous for championing
C*  enter text line #2
U*  the peanut, once remarked that a weed was only a
C*  enter text line #3
U*  vegetable growing in the wrong place.
C*  .
U*  .
    .
    .
    .
C*  enter text line # ...
U*  /
C*  creation complete
    zugzug contains ... lines of text
    press any key to return to menu
```

If the user selects activity 2, 3, or 4, an encryption activity, the dialog should be:

```
C*  ENCODE USING .... CODE

    enter name of file to be ENcoded
U*  zugzug
C*  enter name of file to be created during ENcryption
U*  zotzot
```

After this initial dialog, each encryption subroutine has its own dialog. Activity 2, the cyclic prime code, produces this dialog:

```
C*   input prime number < 38
U*   37
C*   input a number between 1 & 38
U*   17
C*   (after a lot of disk accesses)
     zotzot contains ... lines of text
     zugzug contains ... lines of encoded text
     delete zotzot to ensure security
     remember prime number 37 & number 17
     press any key to return
```

Activity 3, the phrase key code, produces a different dialog.

```
C*   input secret phrase
U*   platypi and echidnae
C*   (after a lot of disk accesses)
     zotzot contains ... lines of text
     zugzug contains ... lines of encoded text
     delete zotzot to ensure security
     remember secret phrase platypi and echidnae
     press any key to return
```

Activity 4, the rail-fence code, has this dialog:

```
C*   (after a lot of disk accesses)
     zotzot contains ... lines of text
     zugzug contains ... lines of encoded text
     delete zotzot to ensure security
     press any key to return
```

When the user selects any of the decoding activities 5, 6, or 7, a mirror image of the dialog above is produced. For example, activity 5, the cyclic prime code, produces this dialog:

```
C*  DECODE USING cyclic prime CODE
    enter name of file to be DEcoded
U*  zugzug
C*  enter name of file to be created during decryption
U*  zoop
C*  input prime number < 38
U*  37
C*  input a number between 1 & 38
U*  17
C*  (after a lot of disk accesses)
    zugzug contains ... lines of text
    zoop contains ... lines of decoded text
    press any key to return
```

Notice that the file zoop has been created to store the cleartext that results from the decryption of the encoded text in the file zugzug. You may consider this process in stepwise fashion:

create file zotzot with cleartext
encode file zotzot, store encrypted text into zugzug
delete zotzot to secure the information
decode file zugzug, store decrypted text into zoop
display zoop to see cleartext

Storage

This system of file protection relies heavily on the use of sequential files for storage of the original text, its encoded version, and the cleartext resulting from its decryption. Aside from the text itself, the files contain no information. Thus the security of the system is enhanced by having all password information in the user's mind and never on file for unwarranted retrieval.

The sequential file storage technique was chosen because of its simplicity and directness. At no time will the user need to retrieve a single line of text without retrieving all the others in sequence, so the sequential file structure is naturally suitable. The individual file records consist of a string surrounded by double quotes.

The menu is managed as an array that is read in from DATA statements into the string array M$. This procedure allows easy changes to the menu in case there should be future embellishments to this file protection system.

Processing

PSEUDOCODE

```
1.   Read menu into M$.
2.   Display menu.
3.   Get user's response W.
     If 1, create text file
           (call create text file subroutine: 3.1)
     If 2–7, encode or decode
           (call appropriate subroutine: 3.2-3.7)
     If 8, display text file
           (call view text file subroutine: 3.8)
     If 9, stop
4.   Upon return from any subroutine go to step 2.
3.1.  Create text file subroutine.
      a. Get name of file from user
      b. Dountil text line from user is "/":
            Get text line from user
            Store text line in file
         Enddo
      c. Display count of lines stored
      d. Return
3.2.  Cyclic prime encoding subroutine.
      a. Open both source and code files
         (call prompt & open files subroutine)
      b. Get prime number 1–38 from user
      c. Get password number 1–38 from user
      d. Encode the text and store in code file
         (call cyclic prime code subroutine)
      e. Cue user to remember both numbers
      f. Return
3.3.  Phrase key encoding subroutine.
      a. Open both source and code files
         (call prompt & open files subroutine)
      b. Get key phrase from user
```

c. Encode the text and store in code file (call phrase key code subroutine)
d. Cue user to remember the key phrase
e. Return

3.4. Rail-fence encoding subroutine.
a. Open both source and code files (call prompt & open files subroutine)
b. Encode the text and store in code file (call rail-fence code subroutine)
c. Return

3.5. Cyclic prime decoding subroutine.
a. Open both code and cleartext files (call prompt & open files subroutine)
b. Get prime number and key from user
c. Decode text and store in cleartext file (call cyclic prime code subroutine)
d. Return

3.6. Phrase key decoding subroutine.
a. Open both code and cleartext files (call prompt & open files subroutine)
b. Get key phrase from user
c. Decode text and store in cleartext file (call phrase key code subroutine)
d. Return

3.7. Rail-fence decoding subroutine.
a. Open both code and cleartext files (call prompt & open files subroutine)
b. Decode text and store in cleartext file (call rail-fence key code subroutine)
c. Return

3.8. View text file subroutine.
a. Get name of file from the user
b. Open the file
c. Dountil end-of-file:
    Input a record
    Display record number and record
  Enddo
d. Return

Code

PROGRAM LISTING:

```
10 ' program : file protection : SS2MOTH3
20 ' authors : JOHN P GRILLO & JD ROBERTSON
30 '
40 CLEAR 1000
50 DIM M$(10)
60 READ M
70 FOR I=1 TO M
80    READ M$(I)
90 NEXT I
100 DATA 9
110 DATA "create text file"
120 DATA "encode text file using cyclic prime code"
130 DATA "encode text file using phrase key code"
140 DATA "encode text file using rail-fence code"
150 DATA "decode text file using cyclic prime code"
160 DATA "decode text file using phrase key code"
170 DATA "decode text file using rail-fence code"
180 DATA "view text file"
190 DATA "terminate processing"
200 CLS
210 PRINT TAB(9);"FILE PROTECTION SYSTEM"
220 PRINT TAB(9);STRING$(50,"-")
230 PRINT
240 FOR I=1 TO M
250   PRINT TAB(10);I;"  ";M$(I)
260 NEXT I
270 PRINT
280 PRINT TAB(9);STRING$(50,"-")
290 PRINT
300 INPUT "         which of the above would you like to do";W
310 IF(W<1) OR (W>M) THEN 200
320 CLS
330 ON W GOSUB 5000,5500,6000,6500,7000,7500,8000,8500,9000
340 GOTO 200
1000 ' **** cyclic prime code
1010 K8=K-P : L8=LEN(S$)
1020 IF L8-INT(L8/P)*P=0 THEN L8=L8+1
1030 S8$=STRING$(L8," ")
1040 FOR I8=1 TO L8
1050    K8=K8+P
1060    IF K8>L8 THEN K8=K8-L8
1070    IF N=1
          THEN MID$(S8$,I8,1)=MID$(S$,K8,1)
          ELSE MID$(S8$,K8,1)=MID$(S$,I8,1)
1080 NEXT I8
1090 S$=S8$
1100 RETURN
```

PROGRAM LISTING (CONTINUED):

```
2000 ' **** phrase key code
2010 V$=" abcdefghijklmnopqrstuvwxyz0123456789"
2020 GOSUB 4000    ' <<<< call string clean-up & compress
2030 J8=0
2040 FOR I8=1 TO LEN(S$)
2050    J8=J8+1
2060    IF J8>LEN(P$) THEN J8=1
2070    S8=INSTR(V$,MID$(S$,I8,1))
2080    IF N=1
          THEN S8=S8+INSTR(V$,MID$(P$,J8,1))+10 :
               IF S8>37 THEN S8=S8-37 ELSE 2090
          ELSE S8=S8-INSTR(V$,MID$(P$,J8,1))-10 :
               IF S8<=0 THEN S8=S8+37
2090    MID$(S$,I8,1)=MID$(V$,S8,1)
2100 NEXT I8
2110 RETURN
3000 ' **** rail-fence code
3010 L8=LEN(S$)
3020 IF L8<>INT(L8/2)*2
       THEN S$=S$+" " : L8=L8+1
3030 S8$=STRING$(L8," ")
3040 M8=L8/2 : J8=0
3050 FOR I8=1 TO L8 STEP 2
3060    J8=J8+1
3070    IF N=1
          THEN MID$(S8$,I8,1)=MID$(S$,J8,1) :
               MID$(S8$,I8+1,1)=MID$(S$,J8+M8,1)
          ELSE MID$(S8$,J8,1)=MID$(S$,I8,1) :
               MID$(S8$,J8+M8,1)=MID$(S$,I8+1,1)
3080 NEXT I8
3090 S$=S8$
3100 RETURN
4000 ' #### string clean-up & compress
4010 S8$=""
4020 FOR I8=1 TO LEN(S$)
4030    IF INSTR(V$,MID$(S$,I8,1))<>0
          THEN S8$=S8$+MID$(S$,I8,1)
4040 NEXT I8
4050 S$=S8$
4060 RETURN
```

PROGRAM LISTING (CONTINUED):

```
5000 ' **** create text file
5010 Q8$=CHR$(34)
5020 PRINT "CREATE TEXT FILE"
5030 PRINT
5040 INPUT "enter name of text file to be created";C8$
5050 OPEN "O",1,C8$
5060 FOR I8=1 TO 1000
5070    PRINT
5080    PRINT "enter text line #";I8
5090    LINEINPUT "?";I$
5100    IF I$="/" THEN 5130
5110    PRINT #1,Q8$;I$;Q8$
5120 NEXT I8
5130 PRINT
5140 PRINT "creation complete"
5150 PRINT C8$;" contains";I8-1;"lines of text"
5160 CLOSE 1
5170 PRINT
5180 PRINT "any key to return to menu..."
5190 IF INKEY$<>"" THEN RETURN ELSE 5190
5500 ' **** encode text file using cyclic prime code
5510 N$="CYCLIC PRIME" : N=1
5520 GOSUB 9500    ' <<<< call prompt & open files
5530 Q8$=CHR$(34)
5540 PRINT
5550 INPUT "input prime number < 38";P
5560 PRINT
5570 INPUT "input a number between 1 & 38";K
5580 PRINT
5590 FOR H8=1 TO 1000
5600    IF EOF(1) THEN 5660
5610    INPUT #1,S$
5620    GOSUB 1000    ' <<<< call cyclic prime code
5630    PRINT #2,Q8$;S$;Q8$
5640    PRINT H8,
5650 NEXT H8
5660 PRINT : PRINT
5670 PRINT C$;" contains";H8-1;"lines of text"
5680 PRINT
5690 PRINT D$;" contains";H8-1;"lines of encoded text"
5700 PRINT
5710 PRINT "delete ";C$;" to ensure security"
5720 PRINT
5730 PRINT "remember prime number";P;"& number";K
5740 CLOSE 1,2
5750 PRINT
5760 PRINT "any key to return to menu..."
5770 IF INKEY$<>"" THEN RETURN ELSE 5770
```

PROGRAM LISTING (CONTINUED):

```
6000 ' **** encode text file using phrase key code
6010 N$="PHRASE KEY" : N=1
6020 GOSUB 9500    ' <<<< call prompt & open files
6030 Q8$=CHR$(34)
6040 PRINT
6050 INPUT "input secret phrase";P$
6060 PRINT
6070 FOR H8=1 TO 1000
6080    IF EOF(1) THEN 6140
6090    INPUT #1,S$
6100    GOSUB 2000    ' <<<< call phrase key code
6110    PRINT #2,Q8$;S$;Q8$
6120    PRINT H8,
6130 NEXT H8
6140 PRINT : PRINT
6150 PRINT C$;" contains";H8-1;"lines of text"
6160 PRINT
6170 PRINT D$;" contains";H8-1;"lines of encoded text"
6180 PRINT
6190 PRINT "delete ";C$;" to ensure security"
6200 PRINT
6210 PRINT "remember secret phrase, ";P$
6220 CLOSE 1,2
6230 PRINT
6240 PRINT "any key to return to menu..."
6250 IF INKEY$<>"" THEN RETURN ELSE 6250
6500 ' **** encode text file using rail-fence code
6510 N$="RAIL-FENCE" : N=1
6520 GOSUB 9500    ' <<<< call prompt & open files
6530 Q8$=CHR$(34)
6540 PRINT
6550 FOR H8=1 TO 1000
6560    IF EOF(1) THEN 6620
6570    INPUT #1,S$
6580    GOSUB 3000    ' <<<< call rail-fence code
6590    PRINT #2,Q8$;S$;Q8$
6600    PRINT H8,
6610 NEXT H8
6620 PRINT : PRINT
6630 PRINT C$;" contains";H8-1;"lines of text"
6640 PRINT
6650 PRINT D$;" contains";H8-1;"lines of encoded text"
6660 PRINT
6670 PRINT "delete ";C$;" to ensure security"
6680 CLOSE 1,2
6690 PRINT
6700 PRINT "any key to return to menu..."
6710 IF INKEY$<>"" THEN RETURN ELSE 6710
```

PROGRAM LISTING (CONTINUED):

```
7000 ' **** decode text file using cyclic prime code
7010 N$="CYCLIC PRIME" : N=0
7020 GOSUB 9500    ' <<<< call prompt & open files
7030 Q8$=CHR$(34)
7040 PRINT
7050 INPUT "input prime number < 38";P
7060 PRINT
7070 INPUT "input a number between 1 & 38";K
7080 PRINT
7090 FOR H8=1 TO 1000
7100    IF EOF(1) THEN 7160
7110    INPUT #1,S$
7120    GOSUB 1000    ' <<<< call cyclic prime code
7130    PRINT #2,Q8$;S$;Q8$
7140    PRINT H8,
7150    NEXT H8
7160 PRINT : PRINT
7170 PRINT C$;" contains";H8-1;"lines of text"
7180 PRINT
7190 PRINT D$;" contains";H8-1;"lines of decoded text"
7200 CLOSE 1,2
7210 PRINT
7220 PRINT "any key to return to menu..."
7230 IF INKEY$<>"" THEN RETURN ELSE 7230
7500 ' **** decode text file using phrase key code
7510 N$="PHRASE KEY" : N=0
7520 GOSUB 9500    ' <<<< call prompt & open files
7530 Q8$=CHR$(34)
7540 PRINT
7550 INPUT "input secret phrase";P$
7560 PRINT
7570 FOR H8=1 TO 1000
7580    IF EOF(1) THEN 7640
7590    INPUT #1,S$
7600    GOSUB 2000    ' <<<< call phrase key code
7610    PRINT #2,Q8$;S$;Q8$
7620    PRINT H8,
7630 NEXT H8
7640 PRINT : PRINT
7650 PRINT C$;" contains";H8-1;"lines of text"
7660 PRINT
7670 PRINT D$;" contains";H8-1;"lines of decoded text"
7680 CLOSE 1,2
7690 PRINT
7700 PRINT "any key to return to menu..."
7710 IF INKEY$<>"" THEN RETURN ELSE 7710
```

PROGRAM LISTING (CONTINUED):

```
8000 ' **** decode text file using rail-fence code
8010 N$="RAIL-FENCE" : N=0
8020 GOSUB 9500    ' <<<< call prompt & open files
8030 Q8$=CHR$(34)
8040 PRINT
8050 FOR H8=1 TO 1000
8060    IF EOF(1) THEN 8120
8070    INPUT #1,S$
8080    GOSUB 3000    ' <<<< call rail-fence code
8090    PRINT #2,Q8$;S$;Q8$
8100    PRINT H8,
8110 NEXT H8
8120 PRINT : PRINT
8130 PRINT C$;" contains";H8-1;"lines of text"
8140 PRINT
8150 PRINT D$;" contains";H8-1;"lines of decoded text"
8160 CLOSE 1,2
8170 PRINT
8180 PRINT "any key to return to menu..."
8190 IF INKEY$<>"" THEN RETURN ELSE 8190
8500 ' **** view text file
8510 P8$="## %"+STRING$(58," ")+"%"
8520 PRINT "VIEW TEXT FILE"
8530 PRINT
8540 INPUT "enter name of text file to be viewed";C$
8550 CLS
8560 OPEN "I",1,C$
8570 FOR I8=1 TO 1000
8580    IF EOF(1) THEN 8630
8590    IF I8-INT(I8/15)*15=0
          THEN IF INKEY$=""
                THEN 8590 ELSE CLS
8600    INPUT #1,I$
8610 PRINT USING P8$;I8;I$
8620 NEXT I8
8630 IF INKEY$="" THEN 8630
8640 PRINT
8650 PRINT "viewing complete"
8660 PRINT C$;" contains";I8-1;"lines of text"
8670 CLOSE 1
8680 PRINT
8690 PRINT "any key to return to menu..."
8700 IF INKEY$<>"" THEN RETURN ELSE 8700
8710 RETURN
```

PROGRAM LISTING (CONTINUED):

```
9000 ' **** terminate processing
9010 PRINT "TERMINATE PROCESSING OF FILE PROTECTION SYSTEM"
9020 FOR I8=1 TO 12
9030    PRINT TAB(3*I8);"."
9040 NEXT I8
9050 STOP
9500 ' **** prompt & open files
9510 P8$=MID$("DEEN",N+N+1,2)
9520 CLS
9530 PRINT P8$+"CODE USING "+N$+" CODE"
9540 PRINT
9550 PRINT "enter name of file to be "+P8$+"coded";
9560 INPUT C$
9570 PRINT
9580 PRINT "enter name of file to be created during ";
9590 PRINT P8$+"CRYPTION";
9600 INPUT D$
9610 OPEN "I",1,C$
9620 OPEN "O",2,D$
9630 RETURN
9999 END
```

TEST AND RUN

PROGRAM OUTPUT:

```
          FILE PROTECTION SYSTEM
          ------------------------------------------------

             1    create text file
             2    encode text file using cyclic prime code
             3    encode text file using phrase key code
             4    encode text file using rail-fence code
             5    decode text file using cyclic prime code
             6    decode text file using phrase key code
             7    decode text file using rail-fence code
             8    view text file
             9    terminate processing

          ------------------------------------------------

          which of the above would you like to do? 1
CREATE TEXT FILE

enter name of text file to be created? peppers

enter text line # 1
?peppers are classified in two groups: sweet and hot.

enter text line # 2
?many people aren't aware of the fact that 'green peppers'

enter text line # 3
?are merely red sweet peppers that haven't fully ripened.

enter text line # 4
?/

creation complete
peppers contains 3 lines of text

any key to return to menu...

          which of the above would you like to do? 8
VIEW TEXT FILE

enter name of text file to be viewed? peppers/txt
 1 peppers are classified in two groups: sweet and hot.
 2 many people aren't aware of the fact that 'green peppers'
 3 are merely red sweet peppers that haven't fully ripened.

viewing complete
peppers/txt contains 3 lines of text

any key to return to menu...
```

PROGRAM OUTPUT (CONTINUED):

```
        FILE PROTECTION SYSTEM
        --------------------------------------------------

          1   create text file
          2   encode text file using cyclic prime code
          3   encode text file using phrase key code
          4   encode text file using rail-fence code
          5   decode text file using cyclic prime code
          6   decode text file using phrase key code
          7   decode text file using rail-fence code
          8   view text file
          9   terminate processing

        --------------------------------------------------

        which of the above would you like to do? 2
ENCODE USING CYCLIC PRIME CODE

enter name of file to be ENcoded? peppers

enter name of file to be created during ENCRYPTION? peppers/cpc

input prime number < 38? 17

input a number between 1 & 38? 12

 1              2               3

peppers contains 3 lines of text

peppers/cpc contains 3 lines of encoded text

delete peppers to ensure security

remember prime number 17 & number 12

any key to return to menu...

        FILE PROTECTION SYSTEM
        --------------------------------------------------

          1   create text file
          2   encode text file using cyclic prime code
          3   encode text file using phrase key code
          4   encode text file using rail-fence code
          5   decode text file using cyclic prime code
          6   decode text file using phrase key code
          7   decode text file using rail-fence code
          8   view text file
          9   terminate processing

        --------------------------------------------------

        which of the above would you like to do? 8
VIEW TEXT FILE
```

```
enter name of text file to be viewed? peppers/cpc
 1  onewart a t nesier wedspe pi:efspip.sutsooarhlg c d
 2  tepra''aee r ahsnfplfgywtre  po'na ereno  a tpaheeetmtcp
 3 r lrptreandh lef  edsti slee'aeheetyep etve aryrumpn.w p

viewing complete
peppers/cpc contains 3 lines of text

any key to return to menu...

         FILE PROTECTION SYSTEM
         --------------------------------------------------

           1   create text file
           2   encode text file using cyclic prime code
           3   encode text file using phrase key code
           4   encode text file using rail-fence code
           5   decode text file using cyclic prime code
           6   decode text file using phrase key code
           7   decode text file using rail-fence code
           8   view text file
           9   terminate processing

         --------------------------------------------------

         which of the above would you like to do? 5
DECODE USING CYCLIC PRIME CODE

enter name of file to be DEcoded? peppers/cpc

enter name of file to be created during DECRYPTION? peppers/txt

input prime number < 38? 17

input a number between 1 & 38? 12

 1              2              3

peppers/cpc contains 3 lines of text

peppers/txt contains 3 lines of decoded text

any key to return to menu...
```

Documentation

NOTES:

Lines 10–340 initialize the variables and manage the menu display. Each line of the menu is stored in DATA statements as a string, allowing for easy alteration of either the menu item or its method of display.

Since lines 1000–4060 are taken up with the coding and string cleanup subroutines, the ON-GOSUB in line 330 performs the appropriate activity in subroutines numbered 5000 and above.

Lines 5000–5770 allow the user to create a text file to be manipulated by the encode and decode subroutines.

Lines 6000–8190 are the encode and decode drivers. They call the appropriate subroutines as the user demands.

Lines 8500–9620 deal with the file of data that the user creates.

CHAPTER

14

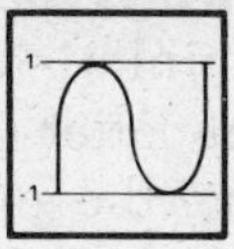

CHEBYSHEV POLYNOMIAL PLOTTER

Introduction

The fourth mother program demonstrates Horner's method for evaluating polynomial equations using graphic output as a basis for clarity of exposition. The Chebyshev polynomials are used here to introduce this class of functions that are so widely used in numerical analysis applications. We chose to use these polynomials in this program to demonstrate how the plotting subroutine can illustrate abstract concepts. The graphic output clearly shows the relationship between these polynomials and their increasing complexity.

Mother Program 4: Chebyshev Polynomial Plotter

User's Problem Statement

Chebyshev polynomials consist of those that produce the successively higher order polynomials $y=1$, $y=x$, $y=2x^2 - 1$, $y=4x^3 - 3x$,

$y=8x^4-8x^2+1$, and so on. This program plots each one of those polynomials in order. The Chebyshev polynomials are useful in numerical analysis when an approximation is desired that keeps the maximum error to a minimum. This is known as the minimax principle. The other commonly used procedure for minimizing errors in approximations is the least-squares method, but the latter can allow extreme errors.

Chebyshev polynomials have the property of having a minimum value of –1 and a maximum value of +1. This property allows them to be plotted without resorting to normalization.

Structure Chart

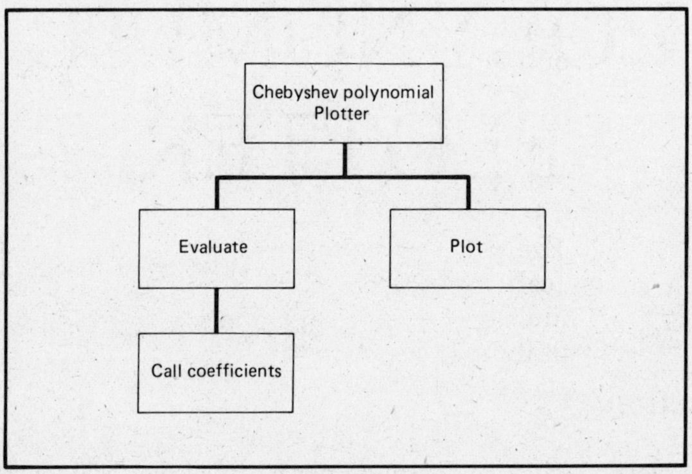

Output Design

For each Chebyshev polynomial a graph is produced ranging from –1 to +1 in steps of 0.5 on the X axis and from 1 to 41 in steps of 1 on the Y axis.

Inputs

None.

Storage

The Chebyshev coefficients are stored in a 10-by-10 array. The X and Y plotting points are stored temporarily in 41-item-long lists during processing.

Processing

PSEUDOCODE

```
1.  Generate the Chebyshev coefficients
    (call Chebyshev polynomial coefficients
    subroutine)
2.  Define X from X(1) to X(41) to range from
    –1 to +1 in steps of 0.5
3.  For I=1 to 9 do:
       For J=1 to 41 do:
          Evaluate this polynomial
          (call Horner's method)
       Enddo
       Plot these points
       (call X-Y plot)
    Enddo.
```

CODE

PROGRAM LISTING:

```
10 ' program : Chebyshev polynomial plotter : SS2MOTH4
20 ' authors : JOHN P GRILLO & JD ROBERTSON
30 '
40 DIM A(10),T(10,10),X(41),Y(41)
50 GOSUB 2000    ' <<<< call Chebyshev polynomial coefficients
60 FOR I=1 TO 41
70    X(I)=(I-1)/20-1
80 NEXT I
90 FOR I=0 TO 9
100   FOR J=1 TO I+1
110      A(J)=T(I,J)
120   NEXT J
130   N=I
140   FOR J=1 TO 41
150      X=X(J)
160      GOSUB 1000    ' <<<< call Horner's method
170      Y(J)=P
180   NEXT J
190   PRINT "T";I;"(x)" : PRINT
200   N=41 : C$="o"
210   GOSUB 3000    ' <<<< call X-Y plot
220   PRINT : PRINT : PRINT
230 NEXT I
240 STOP
1000 ' **** Horner's method
1010 P=A(N+1)
1020 IF N=0 THEN RETURN
1030 FOR I8=N TO 1 STEP -1
1040    P=A(I8)+X*P
1050 NEXT I8
1060 RETURN
2000 ' **** Chebyshev polynomial coefficients
2010 FOR I8=0 TO 10
2020    FOR J8=0 TO 10
2030       T(I8,J8)=0
2040    NEXT J8
2050 NEXT I8
2060 T(0,1)=1 : T(1,2)=1
2070 FOR I8=2 TO 9
2080    FOR J8=1 TO I8+1
2090       T(I8,J8)=2*T(I8-1,J8-1)-T(I8-2,J8)
2100    NEXT J8
2110 NEXT I8
2120 RETURN
```

PROGRAM LISTING (CONTINUED):

```
3000 ' **** X-Y plot
3010 Y8=Y(1) : Y9=Y(1)
3020 FOR I8=2 TO N
3030    IF Y(I8)<Y8 THEN Y8=Y(I8)
3040    IF Y(I8)>Y9 THEN Y9=Y(I8)
3050 NEXT I8
3060 D8=Y9-Y8
3070 IF D8=0 THEN D8=1
3080 FOR I8=1 TO N
3090    K8=INT(1+(Y(I8)-Y8)/D8*40+0.5)
3100    PRINT X(I8);TAB(10+K8);C$
3110 NEXT I8
3120 RETURN
9999 END
```

TEST AND RUN

PROGRAM OUTPUT:

```
T 2 (x)

-1                                                 o
-.95                                           o
-.9                                        o
-.85                                    o
-.8                                  o
-.75                              o
-.7                            o
-.65                        o
-.6                      o
-.55                   o
-.5                  o
-.45               o
-.4              o
-.35            o
-.3            o
-.25          o
-.2          o
-.15        o
-.1        o
-.05       o
 0         o
 .05       o
 .1        o
 .15        o
 .2          o
 .25          o
 .3            o
 .35            o
 .4              o
 .45               o
 .5                  o
 .55                   o
 .6                      o
 .65                        o
 .7                            o
 .75                              o
 .8                                  o
 .85                                    o
 .9                                        o
 .95                                           o
 1                                                 o
```

PROGRAM OUTPUT (CONTINUED):

```
T 5 (x)

-1         o
-.95                            o
-.9                                          o
-.85                                               o
-.8                                                 o
-.75                                              o
-.7                                          o
-.65                                    o
-.6                               o
-.55                       o
-.5                  o
-.45             o
-.4          o
-.35       o
-.3        o
-.25        o
-.2           o
-.15             o
-.1                  o
-.05                       o
 0                              o
 .05                                 o
 .1                                       o
 .15                                          o
 .2                                              o
 .25                                               o
 .3                                                 o
 .35                                                o
 .4                                               o
 .45                                          o
 .5                                       o
 .55                                 o
 .6                           o
 .65                    o
 .7                 o
 .75         o
 .8        o
 .85        o
 .9                 o
 .95                            o
 1                                                  o
```

DOCUMENTATION

NOTES:

In this case, the output tells the whole story. Each one of the ten iterations through the outside loop of the program (lines 90–230) produces the graph of the next higher Chebyshev polynomial, starting with T(0) and ending with T(9). The technique of interest is used before this loop, however, when line 50 calls the Chebyshev coefficient subroutine. The coefficients are produced using a recursive formula. Each successive set of coefficients is defined on the basis of the previously defined set of coefficients.

REFERENCE:

Louis Kelly, *Handbook of Numerical Methods and Applications* (Reading, MA: Addison-Wesley, 1967), pp. 76–81.

CHAPTER

15

PROBABILITY OF ONE PAIR IN POKER

Introduction

The Monte Carlo shuffle of a deck of cards is demonstrated in this chapter, as are some statistical routines for determining the probability of events that occur at random. The reason we chose to demonstrate the probability of a poker hand having a pair dealt to it was because that calculation necessitates the use of these very powerful routines. When you study this program, you will see several other possible variations, such as the calculation of other probabilities. We hope that you will explore the interesting field of programming a card game also.

One noteworthy subroutine appears in this mother program and does not appear in Part 2 of the book. The hand evaluator subroutine determines whether the five cards that were dealt contain a pair. This is a crucial test for the program to perform, and it is not a trivial one. Notice how we do this here, and you may be able to generalize it to three-of-a-kind and four-of-a-kind recognition.

Mother Program 5: Probability of One Pair in Poker

User's Problem Statement:

The program must do two things: First, it should deal a fairly large number of five-card poker hands and count how many of those hands have a pair. In this problem a pair means two cards of the same value in any hand. Second, this program must produce the theoretical probability of such a pair occurring based on the results calculated from the hypergeometric distribution.

Structure Chart

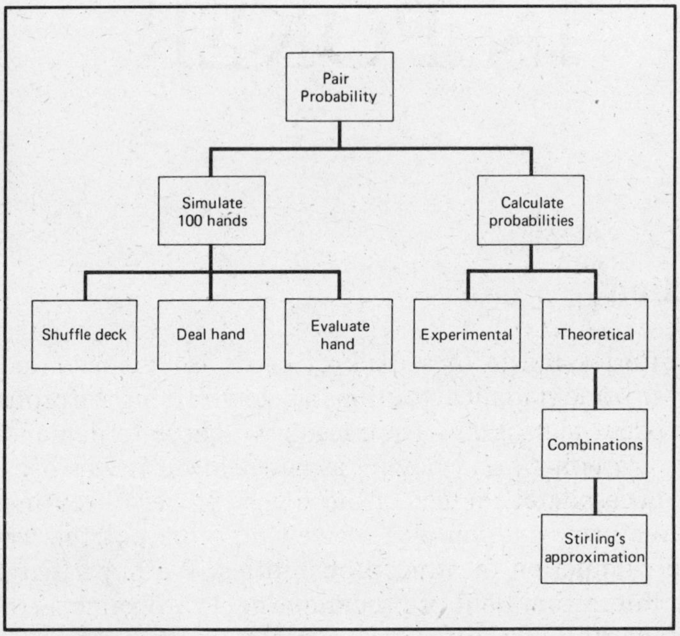

Output Design

The screen displays a running commentary on its success of finding a hand with a pair. As the hands with pairs are generated, they are tallied so that their pseudorandom generation can be compared with the theoretical distribution. When ten decks with ten five-card hands per deck have been dealt five cards at a time, the total tally of hands with pairs is displayed.

The theoretical distribution of hands with pairs is shown next after it is calculated in a separate part of the program.

Inputs

None.

Storage

The string array C$ is reserved for string representations of the 52 cards. The lists C and X are temporary arrays for the cards during dealing and shuffling operations. The array H is reserved as a temporary hand holder.

Processing

PSEUDOCODE

```
1.  For L=1 to 10 do:
      Generate and shuffle a deck
      (call shuffle)
      For i=1 to 46 step 5 do:
        Deal cards 5 at a time
        As hand is dealt, evaluate it
        (call one pair evaluator)
        If hand has pair, display it
      Enddo.

    Enddo.
```

CODE

PROGRAM LISTING:

```
10 ' program : probability of one pair in poker hand : SS2MOTH5
20 ' authors : JOHN P GRILLO & JD ROBERTSON
30 '
40 DIM C$(52),C(52),X(52),H(5)
50 FOR I=1 TO 52
60     READ C$(I)
70     C(I)=I
80 NEXT I
90 DATA "2c","3c","4c","5c","6c","7c","8c","9c","10c","Jc"
100 DATA "Qc","Kc","Ac","2d","3d","4d","5d","6d","7d","8d"
110 DATA "9d","10d","Jd","Qd","Kd","Ad","2h","3h","4h","5h"
120 DATA "6h","7h","8h","9h","10h","Jh","Qh","Kh","Ah","2s","3s"
130 DATA "4s","5s","6s","7s","8s","9s","10s","Js","Qs","Ks","As"
140 PRINT "poker hands with one pair"
150 P=0
160 FOR L=1 TO 10
170     PRINT
180     PRINT "deck";L
190     FOR I=1 TO 52
200         X(I)=C(I)
210     NEXT I
220     N=52
230     GOSUB 1000    ' <<<< call shuffle
240     FOR I=1 TO 52
250         C(I)=X(I)
260     NEXT I
270     FOR I=1 TO 46 STEP 5
280         K=0
290         FOR J=I TO I+4
300             K=K+1
310             X(K)=C(J)
320         NEXT J
330         GOSUB 2000    ' <<<< call one pair evaluator
340         IF S=1
              THEN P=P+1 : PRINT "  hand";(I+4)/5;TAB(10); :
                     FOR J=1 TO 5 :
                         PRINT RIGHT$("   "+C$(X(J)),5); :
                     NEXT J :
                     PRINT
350     NEXT I
360 NEXT L
370 E=P/100
380 GOSUB 4000    ' <<<< call theoretical probability of one pair
390 PRINT
400 PRINT "probability of one pair in poker hand"
410 PRINT "   experimental ...";E
420 PRINT "    theoretical ...";T
430 STOP
```

PROGRAM LISTING (CONTINUED):

```
1000 ' **** shuffle
1010 RANDOM
1020 FOR I8=1 TO N
1030    R8=RND(N)
1040    T8=X(I8)
1050    X(I8)=X(R8)
1060    X(R8)=T8
1070 NEXT I8
1080 RETURN
2000 ' **** one pair evaluator
2010 FOR I8=1 TO 5
2020    H(I8)=X(I8)
2030 NEXT I8
2040 FOR I8=1 TO 5
2050    X(I8)=X(I8)-1-INT((X(I8)-1)/13)*13
2060 NEXT I8
2070 N=5
2080 GOSUB 3000   ' <<<< call insertion sort
2090 S=0
2100 FOR I8=1 TO 4
2110    IF X(I8)=X(I8+1) THEN S=S+1
2120 NEXT I8
2130 IF S>1 THEN S=0
2140 FOR I8=1 TO 5
2150    X(I8)=H(I8)
2160 NEXT I8
2170 RETURN
3000 ' **** insertion sort
3010 FOR I8=1 TO N-1
3020    K8=X(I8+1)
3030    FOR J8=I8 TO 1 STEP -1
3040       IF K8>=X(J8) THEN 3080
3050       X(J8+1)=X(J8)
3060    NEXT J8
3070    J8=0
3080    X(J8+1)=K8
3090 NEXT I8
3100 RETURN
4000 ' **** theoretical probability of one pair
4010 N=13 : M=1
4020 GOSUB 5000   ' <<<< call combinations
4030 A8=C
4040 N=4 : M=2
4050 GOSUB 5000   ' <<<< call combinations
4060 B8=C
4070 N=12 : M=3
4080 GOSUB 5000   ' <<<< call combinations
4090 C8=C
4100 N=52 : M=5
4110 GOSUB 5000   ' <<<< call combinations
4120 D8=C
4130 T=64*A8*B8*C8/D8
4140 RETURN
```

PROGRAM LISTING (CONTINUED):

```
5000 ' #### combinations
5010 X=N
5020 GOSUB 6000    ' <<<< call Stirling's approximation
5030 N8=S
5040 X=M
5050 GOSUB 6000    ' <<<< call Stirling's approximation
5060 M8=S
5070 X=N-M
5080 GOSUB 6000    ' <<<< call Stirling's approximation
5090 D8=S
5100 C=INT(EXP(N8-(M8+D8))+0.5)
5110 RETURN
6000 ' #### Stirling's approximation
6010 S=1
6020 IF X<=0
       THEN S=0 : RETURN
6030 FOR I8=1 TO 10
6040    S=S*I8
6050    IF X=I8
          THEN S=LOG(S) : RETURN
6060 NEXT I8
6070 S=LOG(6.283186)/2+LOG(X)*(X+0.5)-X+1/(12*X)
6080 RETURN
9999 END
```

TEST AND RUN

PROGRAM OUTPUT

```
poker hands with one pair

deck 1
  hand 2      7s   4c   5c   4h   2c
  hand 3      8h  10s   9c   8s   2d
  hand 4      4s   3s   Kh   3h   Qd
  hand 5      9h   Ks   6h   Kd   Ah
  hand 7      6s  10d   Ad   6d   Js
  hand 8      6c   Qs  10c   Jh  10h

deck 2
  hand 1      8c   4c   3h   Qh   3d
  hand 3      7c   Jc   2c   Jh   Kd
  hand 6      5s   Jd   3s   5c   4h
  hand 9      6c  10c   6h   Qd   Kh
  hand 10     Qs   2d   7d   9d   9s

deck 3
  hand 4      7d   7s  10d   5c   4h
  hand 6      4c   4s   9c   3d   8s
  hand 10     Ad   Js   9s   8c   Jh
```

PROGRAM OUTPUT (CONTINUED):

```
deck 4
  hand 2     4h   5h   Qh   Qd   9c
  hand 4     5c   3s   Js   Jh   9d
  hand 6     Kh   8d   8h   Jd   9s
  hand 7     7s   2s   7d   4d   Jc
  hand 9     6h   Ad   As   4c   9h

deck 5
  hand 1    10d   8h   Kh   2h   8d
  hand 2     Kc   Kd   6s   9h   3c
  hand 4     9c   Ad   2d   4h   9s
  hand 5     Jd   6c   Ks   Jc   Ac
  hand 6     Jh   Qd  10h   Js   As
  hand 10    4s   Qc   5h   4d   2s

deck 6
  hand 2     8c   4d  10d  10s   As
  hand 3     3c   5h   Jh   5d  10h
  hand 4     7h   4c   6c   7s   Qs
  hand 7     Jd   Qh   Js   Kd   9h
  hand 8     6h   7d   8s   6s   4s
  hand 9    10c   Qc   Kc   Kh   2c
  hand 10    9d   2d   8h   9s   Ac

deck 7
  hand 2     3h   Jh   As   3d   9c
  hand 9     5c   9s   7h   7s   4h
  hand 10   10c   2d   8h  10s   3c

deck 8
  hand 5     As   Qs   9d   3h   9c
  hand 8     8s   Qc   6d   6h   Jd
  hand 9     Jc   4d   Js   5s   2s

deck 9
  hand 1     5h   9d   5d   7d   8s
  hand 6     8c  10s   6s   Qd  10d
  hand 7     Jc   Kh   Ah   7s   7c
  hand 9     8h   9c   Ac   2h   2s

deck 10
  hand 5     Ac   5h   5c   Js   Ks
  hand 10    4s   Jd   Qh   3d   Qc

probability of one pair in poker hand
   experimental ... .44
    theoretical ... .422572
```

Documentation

NOTES:

The program is somewhat singular in that it has no interaction with its user whatsoever. As it runs, it takes care of itself completely, first dealing 100 hands from 10 decks and counting the pairs in those 100 deals, then calculating the theoretical probability of those 100 deals providing pairs. The only thing left to the user is to compare the two figures—the observed and calculated probabilities.

INDEX